Vocational interests of youth in Ecuador

WYDAWNICTWO
UNIWERSYTETU
ŁÓDZKIEGO

Mariusz Tomasz Wołońciej
Anna Paszkowska-Rogacz

Vocational interests of youth in Ecuador

Inventory of the Occupational Preferences of Youth

Łódź–Kraków 2018

Anna Paszkowska-Rogacz – University of Łódź, Faculty of Educational Sciences
Institute of Psychology, Department of Business Psychology and Career Counselling
Smugowa 10/12 St., 91-433 Łódź
Mariusz Tomasz Wołończiej – The John Paul II Catholic University of Lublin
Faculty of Social Sciences, Institute of Psychology, Department of Experimental Psychology
Al. Racławickie 14, 20-950 Lublin

Published by Łódź University Press & Jagiellonian University Press

First edition, Łódź–Kraków 2018

ISBN 978-83-8088-863-0 – paperback Łódź University Press

ISBN 978-83-233-4420-9 – paperback Jagiellonian University Press

ISBN 978-83-8088-864-7 – electronic version Łódź University Press

ISBN 978-83-233-9790-8 – electronic version Jagiellonian University Press

Łódź University Press
8 Lindleya St., 90-131 Łódź
www.wydawnictwo.uni.lodz.pl
e-mail: ksiegarnia@uni.lodz.pl
phone +48 (42) 665 58 63

Distribution outside Poland

Jagiellonian University Press
9/2 Michałowskiego St., 31-126 Kraków

phone +48 (12) 631 01 97, +48 (12) 663 23 81, fax +48 (12) 663 23 83

cell phone: +48 506 006 674, e-mail: sprzedaz@wuj.pl
Bank: PEKAO SA, IBAN PL 80 1240 4722 1111 0000 4856 3325
www.wuj.pl

Table of contents

Introduction

For most adolescents taking a career decision is usually an overwhelming challenge as they lack necessary knowledge to know where to start a new phase of their path in life, what options they have, and particularly, what they are interested in. They look for the best vocational path that might satisfy their needs and fulfill their expectations. With youth between the ages of 15 and 29 years accounting for about a quarter of the population of roughly 15 million, high school graduates in Ecuador are one of the biggest and fastest growing demographic groups in the country. Country-wide, about 60% of the population is below the age of 29 (INEC, 2010a).

The Economically Active Population (esp. *Población Económicamente Activa* [PEA]) in Ecuador is 4 601 165 persons, of which 1 728 862 are employed full-time and 2 362 396 are employed part-time (INEC 2010a, statistics for March 2010). Recent graduates are usually affected by high levels of unemployment or employment in positions below their educational level or undesirable work places. High school students all struggle to figure out what to do after graduation.

The Ecuadorian labor market is a challenge for young people and working conditions are generally poor, and worse than for adults. In 2009, the employment rate for persons aged 15–24 was 42.9%, as compared to 67.9 percent for adults. The unemployment rate stood at 4.4% among adults and at 14.1% for youth (INEC, 2010b). According to ILO statistics, the employment structure in 2012 in three main sectors was as follows: 27.80% of the Ecuadorian population was employed in agriculture, and this number is growing; 17.80% of employees were in industry; and the biggest group, 54.40%, was employed in the service sector (ILO 2012)[1].

An efficient system of vocational guidance may provide useful information for social policy and for planning future perspectives and recommendations for developments in education and the economy. It may also be reflected in the development of a wider and more accurate educational offer and work options for many social groups, mainly youth.

---

[1] http://www.ilo.org/ilostat/faces/wcnav_defaultSelection?_adf.ctrl-state=k3sz20zlg_4&_afrLoop=89619727883364&_afrWindowMode=0&_afrWindowId=k3sz20zlg_30#! (retrieved 11.11.2015).

Vocational counselors may be able to help youth navigate their careers through the labor market, and with the help of reliable evaluations of the competencies and interests of secondary school students looking for the perfect career with the job that fits best to who they are and who they aspire to be. Hence, this publication aims to support counselors in helping youth to discover their passion and possibly inspire them early, and with current, valid information about vocational interests and the demand in the contemporary job-market help them plan either additional schooling or reaching the job of their dreams.

This work presents a new diagnostic tool: the Inventory of Professional Preferences of Youth in Ecuador (IPPJ – *Inventario de las Preferencias Profesionales de los Jovenes en Ecuador*), with an introduction on how to better navigate their careers efficiently and successfully, taking into account the contemporary socioeconomic context in Ecuador.

The key element of the book is a 15 minute self-assessment tool to help youth discover their professional interests and ideal work. Introductory theoretical and more practical instructive chapters highlight invaluable issues concerning the personality aspects and relevant external ones important in the search and construction of careers that fit students' interests. Both, the tool, with the instructions on how to use it, and the introductory section aim to present what constitutes an appropriate profession choice and how to better match it with a successful job. It also aims to give some practical tips as to whether to confirm a particular choice or seek a new career path.

The book on the occupational interests and *Inventario de las Preferencias Profesionales de los Jovenes en Ecuador* begins with an overview of the socioeconomic and legal context of occupational guidance in Ecuador. The second chapter presents crucial determinants of career choice with significant role of the profession choice. The third section highlights the theoretical assumptions (Holland 1959, 1997; Holland, D. C. Gottfredson, & Power, 1980) of the questionnaire that are the starting point for the validation procedure of the new diagnostic tool.

The fourth chapter presents a detailed description of all crucial steps in the construction of the *Inventario de Preferencias Profesionales de Jovenes* that might serve at first for future, continues the research of academic investigators and experts which is necessary for the development and adaptation of the tool as well as for the longitudinal study of the vocational interests of Ecuadorian students or other related topics and variables. The book was planned as the starting point for further research on the methodology for analysis of professional interests and a longitudinal study to provide a new perspective on the assessment and interpretation of professional interest stability and development.

In the next paragraphs the book presents of the empirical studies indicating the detailed study results of reliability and validity of the tool. An important element of this procedure was the diagnosis of applicability and generalization of John Holland's model in the culturally different and diverse South American context. Hence, the Holland's (1959, 1975, 1992, 1994, and 1997) theoretical model was validated by exploratory factor analysis and confirmatory analysis to discover the internal structure of professional interests in Ecuador and to validate the tool constructed with Ecuadorian vocational counselors.

For the first time a research project on professional preferences of youth entering specific career paths was conducted on a representative national sample. This was made possible through the involvement of more than 4000 individuals: students and a group of psychologists and vocational counselors who participated in the test construction, pilot study, main study, re-test and normalization study.

The fifth chapter describes the data normalization results to provide counselors with useful reference data. Additionally, this section describes in brief the statistical procedure, calculation and interpretation of results. The last section summarizes the methodology and the tool construction process and presents possible challenges and recommendations for the efficient use of the IPPJ questionnaire results in advisory practice in Ecuadorian consulting and educational institutions.

This book on the career preferences of youth in Ecuador has been written as a result of a Prometeo research project of the *Secretaría Nacional de Educación Superior, Ciencia, Tecnología e Innovación* [National Secretariat for Higher Education, Science, Technology and Innovation] (SENESCYT) in Ecuador entitled Occupational Preferences of Youth in Ecuador.[2] The IPPJ is a psychometric tool elaborated in cooperation with a team of 25 psychologists and vocational counselors working as professional counselors in selected Ecuadorian schools (*Colegios*) and advisory institutions, and was coordinated by Mariusz Wołońciej, Ph.D. (Prometeo investigator) in cooperation of Anna Paszkowska-Rogacz, associated professor at the University of Lodz, Poland. The project that resulted in the diagnostic tool was undertaken as a joint venture with the team of specialists representing the SENESCYT, *Sistema Nacional de Nivelación y Admisión* [National Leveling and Admission System] (SNNA), and the *Universidad Central del Ecuador* [Central University of Ecuador] (UCE), as well as institutions dealing with professional guidance and the labor market e.g. the International Labor Organization in Ecuador.

The contributions of crucial actors and decision makers ensured the project's success. This was possible thanks to the institutional support of the SENESCYT, Prometeo project, *Ministerio de Educación, Ministerio del Trabajo* [Ministry of Education, Ministry of Labor], *Universidad Central del Ecuador* [Central University of Ecuador], teachers, and other related administrative entities. We are especially thankful to Lorena Araujo and Pablo Ormaza for their valuable, logistic contribution and expertise, and all persons taking part in the innumerable major and minor tasks, such as collecting data, consulting, and sharing valuable experience and knowledge to improve the investigation methodology and the final publication.

---

[2] The book is an integral part and the guide of the IPPJ questionnaire created during a one-year research project (2014) on the professional interests of youth in transition from secondary school to university in Ecuador.

A supplementary element of the questionnaire is the electronic version of the tool available on the SENESCYT website (http://www.educacionsuperior.gob.ec/) and the manual for vocational counselors. The electronic version allows a student to perform their own self-diagnosis, which may offer them additional information in career planning. After answering the questionnaire items, the student receives a brief report informing him or her of the results obtained related to each of the six Holland model scales.

1. The context of occupational guidance in Ecuador

The number of children in secondary school education has increased tripled in the past ten years, and the number of those registered in superior education has doubled. Though the national project development 'well being' (es. *Buen Vivir*) contributed a lot to the higher education level; it still does not guarantee a quicker or easier integration of youth into the labor market. This may partly result from the low level of education received, or from cultural aspects, but may also be caused by the inadequacy of educational profile choices among academic youth (INEC 2013)[1] as well as poor vocational guidance support for students.

Contemporary, more and less latent labor market indicators highlight some of the challenges Ecuadorian youth face in the transition from school to work as working conditions are poor and generally much worse than for adults. The total official unemployment rate for the general population was low and stood at 4.28 (INEC, 2014)[2]. According to statistics of the *Instituto Ecuatoriano de Estadísticas y Censos* [Ecuadorian Institute of Statistics and Censuses] in 2010 (INEC, 2010b), the employment rate for persons aged 15–24 was high, at around 43 per cent while it was 67.9 per cent for adults.

Interesting, additional markers (e.g. NEET-type indicator) shed light on a hidden dimension of the labor market in Ecuador. A NEET is a young person who is 'Not in Education, Employment, or Training' and is similar to NLFET rate used in 2013 by the International Labor Organization (ILO), where the acronym NLFET stands for 'Neither in the Labor Force, nor in Education or Training'. According to the ILO statistics (see the analysis of the *Organización de Trabajo Decente y Juventud en América Latina* [Decent Work and Youth Organization in Latin America])[3] the NLFET rate in Ecuador is relatively low compared to other South America countries. According to official statistics one in five people between 15 and 24 years of age is neither in school nor working. Simultaneously, the share of young women in Ecuador, from which 32% of the 19–24 age group

---

[1] http://www.ecuadorencifras.gob.ec/estadisticas/ (retrieved 11.11.2015).

[2] http://www.ecuadorencifras.gob.ec/estadisticas/ (retrieved 11.11.2015).

[3] http://www.andes.info.ec/es/noticias/ecuador-tiene-tasa-desempleo-juvenil-mas-baja-america-latina-caribe-segun-gobierno.html#8120 (retrieved 11.11.2015).

neither work nor study, is significantly higher in comparison to men, where 37.1% men have neither any work nor access to education (INEC, 2010b).

Professional education is a significant factor contributing to the average life standards related directly to income levels in Ecuador. An Ecuadorian without a degree earns usually less than 200 USD per month, while a professional who has completed a degree has an income of around 1.500 USD per month (on-line resources de INEC)[4]. Figures show, additionally, that workers with a professional degree often have more and better access to benefits such as training, holidays, social security, etc. than those who have not completed their education (77% vs. 35% respectively).

The context for all these numbers are deep transformations in the Ecuadorian educational system and labor market that have created the need for research that would highlight the role and assimilate the occupational interests of youth and youth career counseling. The mentioned indicators do not necessarily reflect the entirety of the complex situation of youth who need professional guidance on their career paths.

One of the most urgent challenges of the contemporary Ecuadorian labor market is providing new employees with a job that accurately fits their competences, needs and abilities for increased work satisfaction and professional performance. Secondly, there is also a need for the continuous and appropriate adjustment of candidate characteristics to the circumstances of the job environment. Thus, the physical and psychological (i.e., cognitive and emotional) aspects of the candidate should meet the physiological and psychological requirements of the specific job performed (Demerouti, Bakker, Nachreiner, & Schaufeli, 2001).

As mentioned above this study on vocational preferences is an integral and important component of the national program *Buen Vivir* ('well being') program addressed to youth entering the labor market or the next level of their education. Young people, with their specific personality traits, various talents and competence profiles face a critical period of decision-making and the subsequent life-long consequences of these decisions. Thus they are in need of professional support to plan and manage their careers.

The research on vocational interests aims to better understand the real success factors of Ecuadorian students in their post-secondary education and future career. Secondly, it aspires to serve vocational counselors and teachers as a practical tool, which incorporates the necessary theoretical framework for career guidance, and a psychometric tool developed with a representative national sample of Ecuadorian youth (16–19 years old). This publication presents the results of such a study. Both the research methodology description and the questionnaire as a diagnostic tool fill a gap in the system and aim to support efficient human resource management in Ecuador. They may have a direct impact on future job satisfaction, creativity and efficiency at work, and in consequence, the national economy.

---

[4] http://inec.gob.ec/inec/index.php?option=com_remository&Itemid=420&func=startdown &id=935&lang =es (retrieved 11.11.2015).

In the context of contemporary education and the labor market challenges, the *Inventario de Preferencias Profesionales de Jovenes* (IPPJ) may serve Ecuadorian youth as it was designed using the highest methodological standards to ensure its validity and reliability, and in accordance with the complex socio-cultural context of Ecuador in the transition period known as *revolución ciudadana* (citizen revolution).

1.1. New challenges of the labor market in Ecuador

Vocational guidance is an intrinsic aspect of the human resources management process on both a personal as well as societal or national level. Its success is related, among other factors, to the disproportion between the job supply and job demand in the Ecuadorian labor market (INEC, 2010)[5]. At the individual level, human resources management conditions the better use of a given student's personal resources and interests. At the national level, it is reflected in the labor market conditions and results in general life satisfaction in Ecuador.

As the economy in Ecuador is undergoing rapid changes that have deeply impacted the employment structure (INEC 2010a), the educational system is seeking efficient solutions and tools to face future labor market demands. In 2012 according to ILO statistics about 27.8% of the Ecuadorian population was employed in the agriculture sector, 17.8% in industry and 54.4% in the service sector.

An occupational guidance system based on adequate information about the labor market as well as a set of reliable and valid diagnostic tools is capable of providing solutions for the educational system and developing new strategies to support students, graduates and unemployed/underemployed persons, preparing them for the transition into the labor market in Ecuador or abroad.

The Ecuadorian labor market is developing in each of key employment sectors with 36.7% of Ecuadorian population living in rural area and 63.3% in urban regions (World Bank Statistics, 2014)[6]. The situation of youth is especially difficult in rural areas, where Ecuadorians experience very low income and limited employment choice. According to World Bank Statistics the percentage of the population living below the national poverty level is still quite high and this is related to limited education access, low health conditions, economic activity, security, and life satisfaction.

The satisfactory economic indicators of the prior decade are being challenged by the present crisis caused by a growing national debt and very low oil barrel prices in 2015 (oil is one of the key income sources for Ecuador). This situation is aggravated by the disadvantages of the educational system and the labor market situation. The latest indicator of poverty in Ecuador estimated on the basis of

---

[5] http://www.inec.gob.ec/inec/index.php?option=com_remository&Itemid=&func=startdown&id=932&lang=es&TB_iframe=true&height=250&width=800 (retrieved 14.11.2015).

[6] http://data.worldbank.org/country/ecuador (retrieved 14.11.2015).

a population-weighted subgroup from household survey statistics in 2014 was 22.5% of the population. In 2010 the population of Ecuadorians living on less than five dollars a day was 37.1% (ILO Yearbook of Labor Statistics, 2014)[7].

The position of youth on the Ecuadorian labor market scene is somewhat complicated, and contradicts the satisfactory indicators of a relatively low youth unemployment and high employment rate (Figure 1), which do not always coincide with real youth career opportunities.

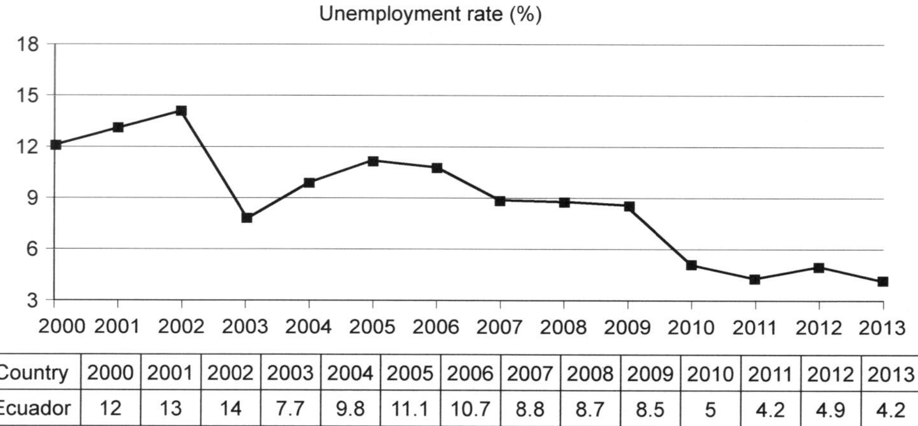

Country	2000	2001	2002	2003	2004	2005	2006	2007	2008	2009	2010	2011	2012	2013
Ecuador	12	13	14	7.7	9.8	11.1	10.7	8.8	8.7	8.5	5	4.2	4.9	4.2

Figure 1. Unemployment rate indicators, 2000 to 2013
(ILO, Yearbook of Labor Statistics, 2014)[8]

According to ILO statistics the unemployment rate is defined as a percent of the labor force that is without jobs and additionally substantial underemployment might be noted. Ecuador has a relatively high Labor Force Participation rate, which was 61.45% in February 2014 (ILO, Yearbook of Labor Statistics, 2014)[9]. The discrepancy by gender was high, however, with female Labor Force Participation at 47.77%. The total unemployment rate in Ecuador was relatively low and ranged about 4.68%,[10] compared for instance to the number of economically active persons without work in Spain during an analogical period of time which was five times higher, 25.9% registered unemployed. As mentioned earlier, the youth unemployment rate (15–24 years old) is also relatively low, as it reached 14.1% in 2009 then dropped to 11.2% in 2011 and 10.2% in 2014. An important characteristic of the labor market is the employment rate understood as the percentage of the total labor force that is employed.[11] Simultaneously, a very

---

[7] http://www.oit.org/stat/Publications/Yearbook/lang--en/index.htm (retrieved 14.11.2015).
[8] http://www.oit.org/stat/Publications/Yearbook/lang--en/index.htm (retrieved 14.11.2015).
[9] http://www.oit.org/stat/Publications/Yearbook/lang--en/index.htm (retrieved 14.11.2015).
[10] With higher Female unemployment was higher at 5,25%.
[11] This may result from the high risk and expense of creating jobs in Ecuador.

high discrepancy in the employment rate between men and women suggests the difference of opportunities between women and men entering the labor market after they complete their education. This is visible in the total employment rate, 50.37%, and only 34.13% from the total labor force related to women.

Taking into account key labor market indicators we may easily overlook some hidden disadvantages in the work environment of youth. The labor market is characterized by a relatively high employment rate and low unemployment, with an employment rate of 46% in the group of youth 15–24 old in Ecuador (Figure 2), while in the European Union it is 32,45%, and in Spain for the analogical group and time it is only 15,6% (ILO, Yearbook of Labour Statistics, 2013)[12]. What is even more crucial marker of the youth condition on the labor market is not only the employment rate but their real opportunities to have education opportunities and vocational counseling to better prepare them for the future successful career.

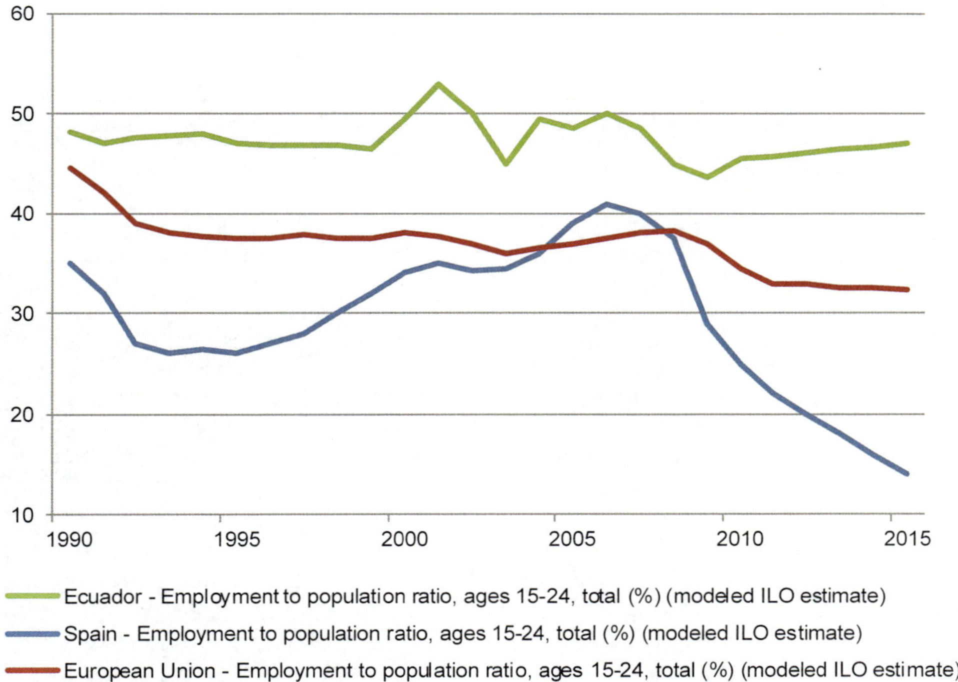

Figure 2. Total employment to population ratio, ages 15–24, in Ecuador: green line (46%) in comparison to the European Union: red line (32.45) and Spain: blue line (15.6%). (Source: ILO, Yearbook of Labor Statistics, 2013)[13]

---

[12] http://www.oit.org/stat/Publications/Yearbook/lang--en/index.htm (retrieved 14.11.2015).
[13] http://www.oit.org/stat/Publications/Yearbook/lang--en/index.htm (retrieved 14.11.2015).

While the employment and unemployment measures seem satisfactory (Figures 1 and 2), youth education rates (Figure 3) indicate disadvantages for future career policy and management as career performance and position in the labor marked is directly linked to level of education (INEC, 2010b). Figure 3 presents statistics based on educational level in 5 groups estimated in the INEC report (2010b):

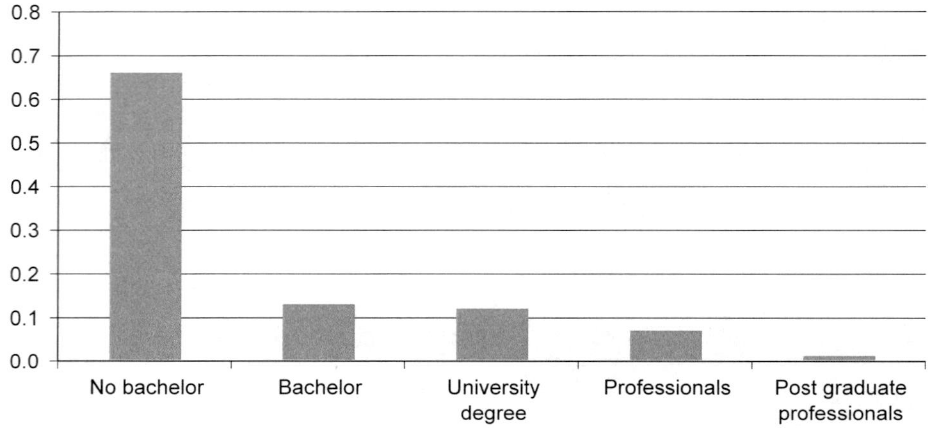

Figure 3. The indicators of 5 levels of educational development in Ecuador
(INEC 2010b)

"No Bachelor": Persons who have not completed secondary education; 2. "Bachelor": Persons who have completed secondary school and who have not gone on to higher education; 3. "University degree": Persons without a higher educational degree who have studied at a level higher than secondary school; 4. "Professionals": Persons with a higher education degree or completing their Master level education 5. "Post graduate professionals": Persons who have obtained at least a post-graduate degree

As indicated in Figure 3, the number of persons who have not completed secondary school (67%) indicates relatively low educational development, which implies significant limitations on future career choices and labor performance and has become one of the major challenges of the society and labor market in Ecuador. The successful adjustment of the employee to the work place depends firstly on the education and skills of the given person, defined by their vocational qualifications. In addition, the deep changes in the nature of work, the continuous re-engineering and work specification process escalated by the automation of work and the shift from low-technology to high-technology activities at workplaces challenges all potential candidates with the high demands of contemporary work performance and specific job position requirements.

Another feature indicated by ILO analysis (ILO, Yearbook of Labor Statistics, 2006)[14] that is related to poor educational markers and consequently the future of the legal labor market is the high number of working children, which complicates the future of youth careers. A report elaborated with the national and World Bank study in 1999 found that 45% of children between the ages of 10 and 17 worked at least part-time. In 2001, 19% of Ecuadorian boys and 11.7% of girls ages 5 to 14 were still employed (Lopez-Acevedo, 2002). The majority of working children were found in the agricultural sector (67.5%). The Government of Ecuador, through the National Committee for the Progressive Elimination of Child Labor (CONEPTI) illustrated the situation of children using the indicator of working children (5–14 years) rate, which was 10.2% in 2004[15], where a majority of working children (71%) were employed in agriculture (flower and banana plantations) and 21% in services. Children are still engaged in the worst forms of labor, as commercial sexual exploitation related with the human trafficking.

Children engaged in labor are in risk of a serious educational but also a social and vocational problem impacting the quality of the future career of youth Ecuadorian. Table 1 provides some key indicators on children's work and education in Ecuador.

Government released the results of the Child Labor Survey from 2013. It indicates that 359 597 Ecuadorian children and adolescents work, which is 8.6% of the population between the ages of 5 and 17.

Table 1. Statistics (2011) on children's work and education in Ecuador (N = 75,689)

Working children in 2011, ages 5 to 14 (% and population)	2.7%
Working children by sector, ages 5 to 14 (%)	
Agriculture	71.0%
Industry	8.1%
Services	21.0%
School attendance, ages 5 to 14 (%):	96.9%
Children combining work and school, ages 7 to 14 (%):	2.4%

Source: UNESCO Institute for Statistics, 2015 "Children's Work and Education Statistics: Sources and Definitions"[16].

---

[14] ILO Convention 182 related to the Prohibition and Immediate Elimination of the Worst Forms of Child Labor.

[15] According to some other NGO organizations e.g. Humanium, in 2004 it was 14% of children between ages 5 and 17 years old worked and not attended a school, and often were victims of a hidden form of domestic work slavery. Though till 2014, Ecuador made a significant effort to eliminate the worst forms of child labor, numbers remain high when looking at child labor done by children under the age of 11. What is pulling a special attention in the situation of children labor is that according to Humanium 56% of child labor involves dangerous occupations e.g. working on banana plantations, where they are exposed to toxic chemicals without any protective gear.

[16] http://data.uis.unesco.org/ (retrieved 05.15.2017).

The Child and Youth legal regulations (according to the new Constitution of October 2008) established the minimum working age at 15, and shaped a general framework for youth jobs directives, including a maximum number of working hours and internship conditions in both the private and public sector. The program 'My First Employment' was launched according to the Government Agenda for Productive Transformation in 2007 to promote capacity building of young people by offering them paid internships (ILO, 2011)[17]. According to government data, 3000 young people have already benefited from this project. Other programs assist specific groups such as young entrepreneurs, returning migrants or researchers and foster the creation of networks of companies, schools and young people.

An adequate career choice depends on one's self-consciousness as well as on basic knowledge about job offers, trends and opportunities of the labor market. The contemporary labor market in Ecuador is marked by continuous changes, which means that persons looking for their place in the labor market or for career options often feel lost. The lack of efficient labor market solutions and vocational guidance as well as the complexity of factors affecting Ecuadorian labor supply and demand significantly lower the effectiveness of young people looking for work, due to insufficient support from educational and labor market institutions. The lack of match in the Ecuadorian labor market is enhanced by the intensive development of certain sectors of the economy, migrations of persons representing certain professional groups or lacking professional education, the decrease in the attractiveness of some professional groups, trends and fashionable jobs. One of the factors affecting the structure of employment is also the lack of a comprehensive labor market needs analysis, which has also resulted in the low and inadequate educational level of persons entering or reentering the labor market (INEC, 2010b).

Effective performance at work depends on the complex combination of an individual's interests, skills, aptitudes, competences, personality features, system of values, physical and health conditions (Athanasou, & Van Esbroeck, 2008; Paszkowska-Rogacz, 2010); these characteristics ultimately define and condition effectiveness in a given profession and concrete job performance. Vocational experts consider occupational interests and qualifications to be the key elements of occupational guidance, linking education resources with the labor market. These standards define all the necessary requirements related to the competences required to successfully perform a given job.

Summing up, despite superficially satisfactory indicators showing relatively high employment and low youth unemployment rates in Ecuador, one may also encounter negative phenomena such as insufficient higher education and underemployment and the omnipresent informal employment in the black market. All these negative trends require even more efficient and professional vocational guidance services for successful careers of youth to increase opportunities and support young Ecuadorians especially while they enter the labor market.

---

[17] http://www.oit.org/stat/Publications/Yearbook/lang--en/index.htm (retrieved 14.11.2015).

1.2. Cultural diversity as a challenge for vocational guidance in Ecuador

One of the possible challenges of vocational guidance is the tremendous cultural diversity in Ecuador. This refers to the ethnic groups living in a particular region of the country and various languages one may encounter, which implies distinct traditions and culture. Cultural diversity encompasses typical customs, languages, traditions, etc., of each of the ethnic groups. The consideration of typical cultural traits of cultural groups especially youth representing different cultural background while entering the education or the labor market. Hence considering all these psychosocial factors is a key aspect of human resources management related to the very high diversity of Ecuador (*Ministerio de Cultura del Ecuador* [National Institute of Cultural Heritage], 2008).

The diversity of cultural heritage of youth refers to their customs, practices, knowledge and mental representations related to the concept of time, human relations, authority and nature. It concerns typical expressions, and all living languages of Ecuador, as well as the system of social values, but also art, myths and rituals, local foods, and traditional medicine that characterize certain communities of the Pacific Coast, Andes, Galapagos or Amazonian Jungle regions (*Ministerio Coordinador de Patrimonio Natural y Cultural* [Ministry Coordinator of Natural and Cultural Heritage], 2008).

This heritage, transmitted in families from generation to generation and continuously recreated by communities in response to their environment, provides youth with a sense of identity and continuity (UNESCO, 2010[18]; (*Ministerio Coordinador de Patrimonio Natural y Cultural* [Ministry Coordinator of Natural and Cultural Heritage], 2008). This cultural background impacts youth-specific behavioral scripts related to their performance in education, the labor market, work environment and occupations.

The cultural and ethnic diversity of Ecuador is best reflected in the number of ethnic groups, native languages and pre-Columbian cultures. 77.4% of Ecuador's population is *mestizo*, which is the heritage of the long lasting interaction between the indigenous and European cultures. There are 13 distinct ethnic groups in Ecuadorian Provinces. The main ethnic communities are: *Chachi* (Esmeraldas), *Tsáchila* (Santo Domingo), *Awa* (Carhi and Esmeraldas), *Epera* (Esmeraldas), *Cofan* (Sucumbios*)*, *Siona-Secoya* (Sucumbios), *Amazonian Quichua* (Sucumbíos, Pastaza), *Waorani* (Sucumbíos), *Zápara* (Pastaza), *Shuar* (Zamora Chinchipe), *Achuar* (Morona Santiago, Pastaza and Zamora Chinchipe), *Shiwia*r (Amazonia) and *Andean Quichua* as well as groups of African descent and montubios (Afro-Ecuadorian indigenous groups of the Pacific coast). Ethnic populations create 20 to 25 cultural communities with different identities as cultural traits, geographical realities and social sets (*Ministerio Coordinador de Patrimonio Natural y Cultural* [Ministry Coordinator of Natural and Cultural Heritage], 2008).

---

[18] http://data.uis.unesco.org/ (retrieved 05.15.2017).

There are 13 native languages. Nine of them are in the Amazonian region: (1) A'ingae used by the ethnic group of Cofan; (2) Coca Pai in the Secoya and Siona ethnic group; (3) Zápara uesd in the Zápara ethnic community. Interestingly, the Zápara language was designated as a world heritage language, declared such by UNESCO in 2001; (4) Shuar chicham of the etnic group of Shuar; (5) Achuar chicham existing in the Achuar community; (6) Wao tededo typical for the ethnic group of Waorani; (7) Kichwa, which is typical for the Kichwa group of the Amazoanian regions (Kichwa del Oriente); (8) Simigae (used by the Kandwash ethnic community); (9) Shiwiar chicham which was the identity marker of Shiwiar ethnic community (Torre, Navarrete, Muriel, Macía & Balslev, 2008).

There are five languages that may be found in the Costa region: (10) Awapit (etnia Awa); (11) Eperapedede (etnia Epera); (12) Cha'palaa (etnia Chachi); (13) Tsafiqui (etnia Tsáchila), and Kichwa spoken by more than three million Quechua-speakers living mainly in the inter-Andean corridor (*Ministerio de Cultura del Ecuador* [National Institute of Cultural Heritage], 2008).

The youth people encounter many not considered challenges while entering educational or labor market institutions as they are in-between the pressure of the modern culture and often ashamed of their heritage and distinct customs, values or language they speak, which should also be considered in contemporary vocational guidance. Culture is one of the most powerful resources in youth guidance; hence it should be recognized and included in multidimensional vocational counseling.

Education in Ecuador is considered to be one of the most important factors of social and economic development according to the national plan. In 2000 the Millennium Declaration was adopted (promoted by the United Nations, the World Bank (WB), IMF and OECD), which includes 8 Goals, 18 Targets and 48 Indicators for 2015. Two of those targets refer to education: completion of primary schooling and gender parity. Adult literacy is missing. In February 2003 the United Nations Literacy Decade (2003–2012) was launched, coordinated at world level by UNESCO, proposing a 'renewed vision of literacy' including children, young people and adults, both within and outside the education system, and throughout life (Torres, 2005). The above advances mask serious problems of quality, efficiency and discrimination in educational provision, to the detriment of public education, the poor in general and, additionally, the rural areas, Indian and black peoples, and the girls and women of these groups. This is evidenced in several quantitative and qualitative indicators, among others (Ponce, 2004).

The percentage of literacy a few decades ago (Table 2) was extremely low and over the last decade it has improved a lot; however, it still requires an effort to continue the long-term reform and increase youth opportunities in the labor market.

The educational infrastructure is quickly developing as the education budget was increased to strengthen development of education; however, it still lacks well-prepared teachers and developed educational programs. The system of education is an integral part of the life-long learning that takes place in the career performance and impacts life and work-satisfaction (INEC 2010b). Children in Ecuador begin basic education at the age of 5 and finish primary school at the age of 12. Education is compulsory until at least the age of 14.

Table 2. Percentage of illiteracy in Ecuador (population of 15 years and over) and average length of schooling (population of 24 years and over)

Year	Illiteracy (%)	Schooling
1950	44.2	2.3
1962	32.5	2.9
1974	25.8	3.6
1982	16.2	5.1
1990	11.7	6.7
2001	9.0	7.3

Source: J. Ponce, 2004 based on SIISE, INEC, censuses of population and housing.

The level of General Basic Education (EGB) is divided into four sublevels:

1. **Preparatory**, which starts with 1st grade of E.G.B. and is usually offered for students 5 years of age;

2. **Basic Elementary**, comprising the 2nd, 3rd and 4th grades of E.G.B. and preferably it is offered to students of 6–8 years of age;

3. **Basic "Medium" education**, which corresponds to 5th, 6th, and 7th grade of the E.G.B., and preferably it is offered to students 9–11 years of age;

4. **Basic Higher Education** corresponding to 8th, 9th and 10th grades of the E.G.B. and preferably/usually it is offered to students 12–14 years of age.

Secondary education comes in 2 phases, each lasting 3 years.

The age limits for compulsory education are from 6 to 14. If students complete their basic education level they can go on to the second level, which is called the General Unified Baccalaureate and precedes higher (University) education. It is comprised of 3 years. The student graduates with a 'Bachelor degree' in the specific specialization. Since 2011 the specialization system has been introduced and the General Unified Baccalaureate is offered.

The aim of the Bachelor Degree education level is to provide a general interdisciplinary education and preparation in order to lead students to the development of life projects and to integrate them into society including their role in the labor market and other social roles. It also aims to develop learning abilities, citizens' competences and prepare them for work, learning and access to the higher education system.

A Bachelor Degree student can choose one of the following options: Bachelor of Science: in addition to the core curriculum, the student has additional training in scientific and humanistic fields. Technical High School: provides additional training in technology, the crafts, sports or artistic areas to enable students to enter the labor market and perform social, entrepreneurial and economic activities. The justification of the need of the Unified Baccalaureate is that is the only way to ensure equality to all high school graduates and to increase the number of optional choices for postgraduates. Thus, completing the curriculum enables students to access higher education in any academic area or directly enter the labor market.

Once the students complete this stage of education they receive a Bachelor Degree. In the case they complete a technical Bachelor Degree they are sent to continue their education in a school with the specified profile. As soon as they complete this level of the education they have open access to University. The Bachelor Degree cycle may lead to higher education. After the Bachelor Degree studies level, education can be continued in a post-secondary university (completed with a Licentiate, Master's title or Doctoral degree) or a non-university school. University studies last from four to seven years, depending on the specialization.

Table 3. The structure of education according to student age,
the year and the level of educational institution

Institutional Level	Basic General Education										General Unified Bachelor Degree			University/ Professional Education				
Age	5	6	7	8	9	10	11	12	13	14	15 or 16	16 or 17	17 or 18	18 or 19	19	20	21	22
Year	1	2	3	4	5	6	7	8	9	10	1	2	3					

Source: Ministerio de Educacion[19].

It is worth mentioning that the expansion of educational provision before the "Buen vivir" reform was not always equal for all, with the rural areas, indigenous inhabitants and blacks being left behind, although the gender gap was closed. The average length of schooling of the national population in 2005 was 7.3 years, but in the rural areas it was 4.9 years – 3.3 years for indigenous inhabitants and 5.9 years for blacks (Ponce, 2004; Torres, 2005).

At present the educational system in Ecuador is gradually being strengthened. Students within the five to fourteen year age group receive mandatory schooling. To a large extent public education in Ecuador is free. However, according to the Ministry of Education in Ecuador, only 10% of the rural population attends secondary level education. Furthermore, only about 76% of the total number of children in Ecuador completes their study through the sixth class (Torres, 2005).

There are 61 universities in Ecuador where students may choose the professional profile of their education. Most of these universities provide degrees of graduation. Post-graduate degrees are also provided by some universities. Universities and other educational institutions also provide various types of post-secondary vocational and technical training.

---

[19] https://educacion.gob.ec/ (retrieved 05.15.2017).

1.3. Ecuadorian youth in the school to work transition

Among the most critical instants in one's career is an adequate assessment of the vocational interests of young women and men and an appropriate career decision. They are significant factors for the successful entrance onto an educational path or the labor market. Mistakes may cause long-lasting and unfavorable effects in their personal lives and society; these also impact the economy. Ecuador is in urgent need of preventive programs that create transparent occupational guidance and decrease the number of ill-made career decisions that have consequences in social dissatisfaction and a lower quality of life, *sumak kawsay* (*Buen Vivir*), which is especially important among youth.

The school-to-work transition is a stimulating time for youth, bringing them new prospects for social and economic independence. However, for a majority of young persons, finding employment is a challenge which they must usually face alone with their doubts, feelings of being lost, and helplessness as to how to become a resourceful worker and member of society. Unfortunately, the transition from one school to another or to work is very often marked by deep frustration and dissatisfaction, while it should be considered to be a time full of hope and self-fulfillment (Bandura, 2001; Weiss, Freund, & Wiese, 2012).

How to prevent failure in this special moment of the school-to-work transition? The school-to-work shift in Ecuador refers to the period ranging from 15 to 24 years of age, depending on the educational system and initial choices related to the future career profile of youth. It may be defined as a critical moment of life when the young person develops skills based on their previous experience (personal and family), formal education and informal or accidental training, all of which helps them to gain necessary competences for a future job.

As mentioned above, some possible and significant aspects of the future career of youth are: personal educational decisions impacted by the educational system regulations, peers and parents. But there are also other less obvious factors such as: general trends and habits concerning employment and work customs in the region of residence (Drabik-Podgórna, & Podgórny, 2006). Apart from these cultural factors there is an important role to be played by inborn abilities, personal interests, the first experience of work performing certain duties and occupations or conversely, inactivity (worklessness or unemployment), seeking their first job, acquiring skills and knowledge that shape future vocational identity, as well as more formal aspects such as: labor market opportunities, necessity of work migration, possible incomes, etc.

The flux of many factors influences the occupational identity of the young person and shapes their future career path more unconsciously than consciously. The complex context of youth decisions related to their work require professional and comprehensive youth policies integrated at the national or regional level,[20]

---

[20] An example of how migration may impact on the labor market and the well-being of youth is the region of Santo Domingo de los Tsachillas. The rapid influx of migrants during the last 4 decades

Institutions related to education and the labor market should support youth in appropriate decision-making and expose students to potential and successful future careers, taking into consideration their personal resources as well as the socio-economic context of Ecuador.

An accurate and reliable diagnosis of the occupational interests of students carried out with professional diagnostic tools provides them with the opportunity to increase their own self-consciousness, self-diagnosis, and finally, enable a valid and adequate life decision related to both education and the career path of the individual. This was the goal of this project.

Effective policy should aim to support the adjustment of the young person in the labor market. Preparing youth for their future jobs requires vocational guidance, while labor market management relies on systemic planning and monitoring of labor market trends, e.g. surplus jobs. Such valuable data may serve to develop the logic behind recommendations for the structure and offer of the educational system and its adjustment to the labor market needs.

While "success" in the student's school to work transition is determined by many factors, both internal and external, the reliable diagnosis of vocational interests provides vocational counselors with valuable information that will help to assist youth to find fulfillment in their future job.

1.4. Youth passivity and work instability in the labor market

The significant level of educational and work inactivity of young people points to their real situation, dependent on the varying effectiveness of regime social policy and the labor market. Measures of this inactivity in education and work complement traditional measures of this group's labor market situation, such as employment and unemployment labor market rates. The difficulties of contemporary young people in work and educational activity have required the introduction of additional indicators characterizing their activity in the economy, which are also applicable to Ecuador. The importance of new labor market measures such as the NEET indicator described below has been confirmed by numerous scientific studies that confirm that inactivity in the early days of professional activity creates many negative consequences in the long term, both at the micro and macro level (Assireli, 2007; Szcześniak, & Rondon, 2012).

The related social problem of youth inactivity is a worrying phenomenon of the growing social category of young people who lack fulltime employment and choose to avoid contracted work, as very often they do not identify themselves with a specific 'own profession' profile. Very often graduates don't enter their career after they finish high school or university and remain in 'inbetweeness,'

(population growth of 40 000 to 400 000) with insufficient social, educational and vocational policies in place resulted in alarming indicators of psychosocial problems among youth, partly related to their career problems: the highest criminality, suicide and depression indicators.

neither in school nor work. The alarming signal of this syndrome, similar to the classically Japanese phenomenon of *freeters*[21] is the European example of the growing number of so-called youth NEETs (Wołońciej, 2012). This acronym refers to young persons who are 'Not in Education, Employment, or Training.'

A similar problem also refers to a subcategory of *NEETs* and is defined in the newly coined *NLEETs* rate used in the 2013 report on Global Employment Trends for Youth by the International Labor Organization. The NLEETs acronym refer to young persons who are 'Neither in the Labor force nor in Education' and demonstrates the less visible and measurable aspects of economic or educational activity of Ecuadorian youth, provides data on the availability, coverage and effectiveness of policies for young people, and indicates the impact of interventions aimed at improving the social, education and employment situation of the most disadvantaged youth.

These disadvantageous phenomena especially among youth and many other more or less visible ones pose a challenge to occupational guidance in Ecuador, creating the need for solutions and preventive programs addressed to youth leaving education and looking for their 'own niche' in the world of occupations. The NEET measure is an indirect indicator of youth vocational policy and an significant signal as to living conditions of youth not in employment, education or training (the NEETs). The percentage of 20–24 year old NEETs in OECD countries in 2013 was 18% (it was 32% only in Spain).[22]

This group is characterized by young persons who are excluded from the labor force, as they are no longer considered to be unemployed. In Ecuador it may be appropriate to estimate real indicators of youth employment and unemployment rates considering hidden unemployment and NEET-like indicators, informal employment such as street-workers or the agriculture sector, and the underemployment of youth.

An additional disadvantage of the contemporary youth careers is very high fluency and job changes at the labor market, especially among youth. Official statistics concerning this phenomenon are still not available, however the precariousness of employment has become a common and omnipresent characteristic challenging the labor market and social security and stability, especially of youth in Ecuador.

The very high fluidity in contracted employment and low level of loyalty of young employees is reflected e.g., in the syndrome of *job-jumpers or job-hoopers*, namely, frequent moving from job to job and from employer to employer (Wołońciej, & Gellert 2009) well-described in Europe.

---

[21] Freeter (in Japanese: *furītā*) The word *freeter* derives from the English word *free* and the German word *Arbeiter* (worker) and denotes young people who lack full-time employment or are unemployed and/or who deliberately choose not to become a 'salaryman' even if they are given a job. It usually refers to the group of young people who do not choose to begin their career after high school but decide to earn a living in low-skilled and low-paid occupations. It has become a common phenomenon among students.

[22] OECD Data, Youth not in education or employment (NEET), February 2014. There are no NEET statistics for Ecuador but, for instance, there were 25% NEETs in Colombia in an analogical group and time.

These trends influence the effectiveness of contemporary vocational guidance to match educational 'supply' with labor market demands, and ensure work productivity goes hand in hand with high performance and life satisfaction of future employees. This publication seeks to respond to the new circumstances of youth entering the world of work, who are challenged by new social demands as well as legal and administrative regulations, and need to consider in an efficient management of their own education path and career choices.

1.5. Need for tools in occupational guidance in Ecuador

The lack of a psychometric tool in occupational guidance in Ecuador is one of the most significant limitations in the quality of occupational counseling of youth preparing for their future job. As mentioned earlier, in line with the work of Super (1984), an important component of professional decisions are preferences, and in particular – personal interests. One of the most commonly known and used diagnostic tools to measure aspects related to professional guidance and interests of Ecuadorian youth is, for example:

Inventario de Intereses y Preferencias Profesionales (López, 2000);

Cuestionario de Intereses Profesionales Revisado: CIP-R (Fogliatto, Pérez, Olaz, & Parodi, 2003);

Inventario Ilustrado de Intereses (GEIST, Geist, 1970);

Inventario Tipologico Temperamental (Bastidas, 2003)[23].

A significant limitation of all these techniques, applied in counseling services in Ecuador is that they were created on the basis of small samples, e.g. as a student's or as teacher's thesis projects, without complete and appropriate psychometric features. Additionally, this is a serious limitation for Ecuador with its high diversity between rural and urban regions, socio-geographic differences between seaside, mountains or jungle areas and finally the very high cultural diversification, with more than 20 ethnic groups. Hence, tools applied in vocational guidance have also not been representative in the context of the variance in sources in this heterogeneous society.

Additionally, a majority of techniques have not been revised, since they were developed 20 or 30 years ago, or they were translated without appropriate cultural adaptation. This means that the content as well as the language of the test and the standards are out of date according to the Tests Standards (*Standardy dla testów stosowanych w psychologii i pedagogice*, 2006) used in psychology and pedagogy. In fact, Holland's (Holland, & Rayman, 1986) test is being applied in Ecuador without the required license. Significantly, the majority of occupational guidance counselors use it as the main tool applied in their work.

---

[23] However the test created by Bastidas Paes in 2003 and used for students and by vocational counselors educated by UCE is based on Holland's model and the model of temperaments but lacks the adaptation, normalization, as well as psychometric indicators.

For these reasons, the project run in cooperation with SENESCYT and SNNA in 2014 is an important and valuable milestone in the occupational guidance development and services provided for Ecuadorian youth (aged 16–19) entering the next level of education or the labor market.

Thus, the development of modern, up-to-date diagnostic tools will support the Ecuadorian vocational guidance system at the secondary school level. While the preliminary plan aimed to include an elaboration of the diagnostic tool of occupational interests of primary school children in the project, after conducting a pilot study of the younger age groups attending primary school (e.g. 12 years old) as well as for obvious developmental reasons, the decision was made to exclude that group because of their low maturity of occupational identity and lack of necessary cognitive skills. Thus the study group was ultimately limited to graduates of the secondary schools (*colegios*). Nevertheless, it is recommended that in the future other techniques such as the commonly used Test of Photos of Professions (*BBT: Berufsbilder Test*) (Achtnich, 1987) be elaborated to accompany younger persons in their career path construction. This test proposed by Martin Achtnich (1979) is a projective technique to identify professional inclination. The test material consists of photos of professionals performing various types of activities that are assessed as positive, negative, or indifferent. That method would be much more appropriate for the preliminary testing of preferences among younger group in the schools at the basic level, e.g. 10–12 years old, or children finishing primary schools.

To respond to the need for tools in vocational guidance in Ecuador a new tool Inventory of the Occupational Preferences of Youth (IPPJ – *Inventario de Preferencias Profesionales de los Jovenes*) has been developed as a diagnostic technique for secondary school graduates and other individuals facing the need to make a choice concerning the future stages of their education and/or work.

That specific choice requires a more detailed analysis of professional aptitude and personal limitations related to the profession chosen. The developed tool is a completely new technique elaborated according to obligatory standard for tests used in psychology. The IPPJ questionnaire was created on the basis of a specific theoretical foundation, the concept of occupational personality and the theoretical model of professional interests by Holland (1997).

1.6. Legal aspects of professional guidance in Ecuador

In Ecuador, as in other European countries or the United States, educational standards guarantee free and common accessibility of advisory services during the educational process in the school, as stated in 2014 in the *Normativa departamento de consejeria estudiantil en establecimientos* (Normative department of student's counseling in establishments) (2014). In comparison, one of the main documents that guide the policy of vocational counseling services in the European Union is *A Memorandum on Lifelong Learning* adopted by the European Commission in. The legal documents list specific regulations for professional development of advisory assistance for students in planning their careers as one of the six main objectives.

Ecuador in line with other countries has specified legal solutions to the career guidance problem to be applied in all relevant institutions. The vast majority of EU countries have applied the recommendations of the *Resolution of the Council of the European Union Guidance throughout life,* which was the result of research and analysis carried out for the European Commission (as cited in Bysshe, Hughes and Bowes, 2002). This resolution was adopted in May 2004, and was accompanied by the most important document issued by the European Union on career guidance (*Career Guidance: a Handbook for Policy Makers,* 2004). The document stresses the importance of carrying out consultancy services in vocational schools for the development of national human resources. Realization of its objectives is the subject of continuous monitoring (*Lifelong Guidance Policies Work in Progress. A report on the work of the European Lifelong Guidance Policy Network 2008–10,* 2010; Bimrose, Barnes, & Hughes, 2008). Contemporary legal regulations in Ecuador may offer a new framework for cooperation of relevant Ecuadorian institutions and entities in the field of education, as they stress the importance of vocational guidance for the implementation of the strategic objective of increasing youth mobility and strengthening lifelong learning to face contemporary labor market challenges. One of these challenges is including the provision of new skills for new jobs that are being created in the educational and professional guidance system.

The implementation of legal regulations obliges all Ecuadorian educational institutions to prepare students for their choice of occupation and field of education. These activities could be implemented by school, psychological and pedagogical entities administered by the Ministry of Education and specialist consulting entities, in the form of individual counseling for students, parents and teachers, as well as various types of group assistance.

According to principles outlined by Ecuadorian legal regulations regarding rules for providing and organizing psychological and pedagogical support in public kindergartens, schools and institutions, directors of educational institutions are obliged to organize an occupational advisory system and the necessary related activities to facilitate an adequate choice of school and thematic profile of education. In this context, schools are expected to increase the opportunities of their students to find efficient and appropriate employment (*Normativa departamento de consejeria estudiantil en establecimientos,* 2014).

The changing labor market, evolution of technology and the transformation of the education system implies that the student is forced to act and plan his/her future in a situation of continuous change. The unstable situation in the labor market causes disorientation, confusion and the feeling of being lost.

All factors mentioned above point to the indisputable need for high-quality professional guidance accessible for all students. The quality and professionalism of the services provided to that specific and demanding group depends firstly on the approach and skills of the vocational counselor, in particular the set of tools he or she uses in their advisory work. Good quality advisory services may be warranted by professional diagnostic tools that provide students with information about their occupational preferences and aptitudes, as well as increase their self-awareness. All these elements are crucial for an accurate educational and vocational decision made by students. High-quality professional guidance services minimize possible costs resulting from inadequate choices and improper planning of the youth.

2. Determinants and correlates of career choice

Occupational reality is an inevitable and unavoidable topic of every person, from the very first moment of life. Occupational interest is directly related to career and is impacted by the complex and constantly changing flux of factors. Each individual constructs their own self-concepts (Super, 1984) that result in specific career interests and impact the most important spheres of life. People try to better navigate their life taking into account all possible key factors of their career course.

Where does one's vocational personality and self come from, and what factors limit or contribute to possible vocational choices? Is career path defined by genes or does it emerge from the socio-cultural context of the young person? Is it the product of nature or nurture? Is it an imprint of socialization or physical environments? And, finally, is our career a predetermined outcome or rather we are active actors determining our future occupational path? The main issue in career choice may be coined in the question, of whether all distinct professional career constructs (Lent & Brown, 2005; Super 1984) are incidental by-products of life events, or the result of our free and conscious construction. Summing up, all possible aspects of career construction are related to vocational consciousness and free choices in professional career.

Interests are both rooted in genes and conditioned by environmental factors that shape personality (Schermer, Petrides, & Vernon, 2015). Genetic factors influence temper, defined as the way one relates to different types of situations, which is reflected in e.g. perseverance, sensorial sensitivity, emotional reactivity, endurance, speed that influence efficiency in different task performance by a given individual (Zawadzki, & Strelau, 1997).

Among many personality traits that are directly conditioned by genes there is also openness to new experience, and specific inborn abilities such as: intelligence, creativity, artistic or linguistic skills, and the like (Paszkowska, 2011). Another significant set of personal determinants are complex environmental variables. Among these factors is the privileged position of the primordial socialization group such as the family, and derivative social groups as school, peers environment, the wider social environment and the labor market. The last area of possible personal and professional interests is related to aspects of personality, the self-concept, the system of needs and values (Bajcar, &Gąsiorowska, 2006; Schermer, et al. 2015).

While psychology as a science has a relatively short history inaugurated by Wundt's psychological laboratory, it has come a long way in the effort to explain what in fact influences human behavior, and in our case, what determines the choice of career (Paszkowska, 2011). Three basic questions lie at the starting point for scientific considerations related to mechanisms guiding vocational development and career planning decision making: (1) Why do people choose or not choose a specific educational and/or career path? (2) Why do they change it at some points in their lives? and (3) How do career preferences change across the life-span in successive stages of development?

Seeking the answer to these tentative questions, researchers such as Krumboltz (1979) and Super (1984) began to identify two groups of conditions that might cause changes in the development of one's career. The main group of factors is situational and external, such as the current social structure, socio-historical changes, socio-economic conditions, natural environment resources and diversity regional tradition, culture and style of work and infrastructure development. Key role in career management is played by the existing procedures of employment policy in the country, the educational system, and socio-cultural aspects such as cultural diversity, ethnic group heterogeneity and migrations. Career development depends significantly on the family, which is treated as one of the most crucial factors requiring special attention among the listed external factors.

The family has a particular impact on decisions and career choices people make, the course of their career, the way people think of success and their professional development. The family environment transmits a multigenerational "message" regarding life style, the concept of work, style of work, conception of time and space as work domains, professional rules, mental representation of work and professional life, prestige and success of the job performed (Wołońciej, 2012). It is in the family that young people learn typical and established lifestyles, develop their interests, acquire their first ideas and knowledge about the family members' professional models, acquire and learn to perform their social and professional roles, and develop a system of values, norms and basic assumptions associated with the interplay of work and personal life balance.

The family is the closest socio-cultural environment where a young person experiences their first successes and failures, and learns how to perceive and define certain situations as a victory or as a defeat. Most contemporary theories of vocational development position family as one of the most influential and important determinants of occupation choice and the professional decisions of youth (Shin, & Kelly 2013).

A second group of factors refers to internal determinants of the individual and are located more in the person than the environment (Schermer, et al., 2015). Internal factors consist of biological factors that may determine special abilities. Biological or genetic determinants very often limit the choice of certain professions requiring specific features and requirements, even if the person possesses all necessary psychological characteristics, such as: attitudes, interests, needs, and a hierarchy of values. That is a difficult and conflicting situation that has to be faced constructively by the decision maker as well as the professional counselor.

Both of these groups of determinants of professional choice, internal and external, operate in mutual dependence, and so the question of what is inherited and what is acquired from the socio-cultural environment is a very difficult one to answer. This chapter presents some selected internal determinants such as biology, external ones such as the family environment, as well as psychological determinants, which are the interplay of both factors and may complement and enrich students' career choices – choices that condition their future work satisfaction. This chapter shows the background of the psychological diagnosis of occupational orientation, which aims to effectively guide the career of the young individual.

2.1. Physical constitution and health in professional choices

In common guides and classifications of occupations one may find some requirements such as: 'a driver needs to have a good general health condition, physical strength, good eyesight and hearing, proper motor skills, and mechanical comprehension skills', and so on. Another example taken from a commonly-used description of professions characteristics is: 'a chemist should have an efficient organ of sight, hearing, smell, taste, touch and balance' and 'no allergies, especially allergy to fur and grass pollen allergy and hay fever is recommended to practice the profession of veterinarian'; confectioners, for example, are forbidden to perform the job with 'chronic hand skin lesions, the lack of binocular vision, limb motor disability' (Lelińska, 2006, p. 210; Paszkowska-Rogacz, 2011).

Limitations of a biological/physiological nature may meaningfully reduce opportunities in the professional choice of the young person, hence are important information always to be considered in the choice of profession. Even slight physical health limitations may make it impossible to perform certain jobs with satisfaction and success. Sometimes it is important to take into account if the person is characterized by sufficient physical strength or health. The development of medicine of work and new techniques permit a thorough health condition examination. In addition, significant medical services are progressing and developments in treatment effectiveness allow for people with even serious diseases to be treated. They have also resulted in the decrease in scale of health problems and diseases that should be considered in the process of professional orientation (Paszkowska-Rogacz, 2011; Wołońciej, 2012).

The advantages of the development of medical services are obvious; they save people's lives, from children with genetic defects from environmental pollution to victims of road accidents and others. This has significantly increased the number of people entering their professional lives with psychophysical limitations or illnesses which by necessity changes and limits their life plans (Kalwij, & Vermeulen, 2008). Important aspects of the assessment of occupational qualifications are the senses: visual, auditory, taste, touch; they are potentially crucial to performance of a specific job. We may observe a positive trend of inclusion of persons with physical or mental disabilities in the labor market that in most cases allows them normal socio-economic functioning (Bambra, & Eikemo, 2009).

The International Labor Organization (ILO, esp.*Organización Internacional del Trabajo OIT*) as well as some Ecuadorian government regulatory bodies such as the Ministerio del Trabajo [Ministry of Labour], Ministerio de Relaciones Laborales [Ministry of Work Relations] or Ministerio de Inclusión Economica y Social [Ministry of Social and Economical Inclusion] (MIES) in Ecuador have developed clear recommendations for necessary requirements in specific occupations. Simultaneously, new legal regulations aim to prevent the social exclusion of people with disabilities, stating the need for integration efforts bringing the problems of people with different disabilities into the public eye. We may also observe the positive trend of growing social acceptance (Stein, 2010) of the active participation of people with incomplete sensory or motor abilities in the workplace. At the same time, the choice of the specific profession in these cases should be well-considered.

Apart from commonly-known and listed health factors, there are some relatively new civilization trends that seriously affect the human health of all age groups and are directly related to work nature and the nature of vocational performance. The rapid development of technology, communication and media (TICs) has resulted in unexpected negative results. A serious detrimental phenomenon is *hypokinesia* defined as diminished or abnormally low activity and slow movement. It is also called hypomotility or immobilization. Insufficient motor activity in the nature of the present vocational spectrum impacts the everyday life of children and youth as well as at the work place and has become a prevalent problem mentioned by the International Labor Organization or World Health Organization (WHO) (Wołończiej, 2012) as one of the most often direct and indirect causes of sickness and death.

The problem of *hipokinesia* comes from an increase in the overexertion of the nervous system, and a meaningful decrease in muscular activity, which results in serious complications such as defects in posture, the audio-visual, cardiovascular, digestive, and autonomic nerves systems, as well as mental health problems.

According to the WHO research analysis *hypokinesis* associated to the obesity and overweight and is closely related to the so called Noncommunicable Diseases (NCDs), also known as chronic diseases, are not passed from person to person. The 4 main types of noncommunicable diseases are cardiovascular diseases (like heart attacks and stroke), cancers, chronic respiratory diseases (such as chronic obstructed pulmonary disease and asthma) and diabetes. NCDs affect especially low- and middle-income countries, such as Ecuador. In this case it occurs in three quarters of all NCD deaths which is 28 million cases (WHO 2014)[24]. In that sense contemporary vocational choices are not only conditioned by good physical health but also became a serious civilization characteristic and matter of physical health of youth.

---

[24] Global Status Report on Noncommunicable Diseases 2014, WHO Library Cataloguing-in-Publication Data (Publication is also available on the WHO website: www.who.int).

2.2. How does temperament influence occupational choices?

Though there are billions of people on our planet, we may encounter remarkable similarities among them. Modern psychological theories have created taxonomies and models that assign all of us to one basic temperament types related to our personality type. What does this mean for youth vocational choices? Helping youth to know who he or she is may contribute much to better understanding the path one chooses through college or higher education and finally, one of many possible career paths.

Temperament is one of the features that noticeably differentiate people in their daily performance and work activities (Keirsey, & Bates, 1984). In line with Holland's (1997) theoretical model of person-environment congruence, temperament plays an important role in effectively navigating one's professional career on the basis of specific personal characteristics (Paszkowska-Rogacz, 2011). Some people are very persistent, for example, while others tire quickly; some react very calmly in difficult situations, while others react quickly and emotionally – in those cases, we say that someone is 'explosive'.

According to Strelau (2006), temperament is defined as the set of specific features of behavior and in comparison with other psychological concepts and phenomena; temperament is characterized by relatively constant individual characteristics across the lifetime. It has a strong biological background, which is why it is relatively resistant to changes resulting from external factors.

Temperament is often considered as the emotional response associated with a general human reactivity and activity (Keirsey, & Bates, 1984). However, temperament is manifested not only in emotions, but also in other mental processes, for example: perception, attention, decision-making process and problem-solving strategies.

It is worth considering the temperament of the candidate seeking work in a particular occupation in relation to the job characteristics. For example, physical or psychic strength would be manifested in the ability to function well during situations of prolonged or severe stimulation. A recommendation or counter indication for an individual to perform a specific job may arise from the significant decrease in optimal psychophysical functioning and safe performance of a specific profession (Kreft, Sołtysińska, Łukaszewicz, & Dankowska, 2000).

If an employee's temperament matches the specific work environment and job conditions, there are no obstacles to choosing and performing specific occupations with their physical and psychological requirements; however the statistical significance of empirically tested relationship between temperament and vocational type is not always confirmed (Oakland, Stafford, Horton, & Glutting, 2001; Paszkowska, 2011).

Vigor and liveliness are important features of temperament that allow employees to maintain a high work rate and adapt easily to changes in the work environment (Oakland, 2001 et al.; Strelau, 1998). These characteristics are essential in professions requiring high responsibility and frequent contact with people, e.g.: waiter, nurse, doctor, teacher, and salesman. Other temperamental characteristics, such as so-called 'cold blood' include carefulness, reflex and responsiveness; they are required in the professions of train machine driver or car driver.

When a person is characterized by high emotional reactivity, that is, a tendency to respond intensively to stimuli, that person should avoid professions where competition, high stimulation, stress and time pressure (such as a police officer, broker, simultaneous translator) is typical in a daily context. Whereas if the employee enjoys 'peace and quiet,' solitude, is patient and careful, he or she will enjoy performing the jobs of programmer, fitter/assembler, archivist, and librarian. If his emotional reactivity is low, and has a high level of activity, seeking highly stimulating actions, likes to move, change, be in the company of people, it may indicate high efficiency in social professions requiring contact with people (hairdresser, nurse, doctor, teacher, flight attendant) or professions characterized by physical danger (fireman, pilot) (Paszkowska-Rogacz, 2011).

The interesting and relevant results of Karwowska-Szulkin and Strelau (1990) as well as data obtained by Eliasz (1981) provide empirical evidence and the confirmation of these assumptions. They show the significant association between the level of temperamental reactivity with the performance of specific professional tasks, and the preference of a particular activity characterized by specific stimulation value. The higher the stimulation value of certain tasks and the greater preference for exploration of such stimulation, the lower reactivity of persons that choose such activity. The context of the undertaken research suggests we may find an answer to the question of whether occupational preferences regarding the stimulation level of different professions may be identified in young people's occupational choices.

A closer analysis of the relationship between the temperament types of youth in Poland and their preferences of professional activities did not find this relationship to be statistically significant (Paszkowska, 2011) however other cross-cultural research is necessary to test it in other societies and in Ecuador. Oleszkiewicz-Zsurzs (1986) conducted a survey of students, asking them to select occupations which they would like to perform in the future, and those they would prefer to avoid in the future. Occupations were selected to represent different degrees of stimulation in social, physical and intellectual aspects. Interestingly, the results revealed no association between preferred professions and the level of emotional reactivity of students. However, when taken into account the negative choices, namely what they would avoid as their possible future profession, the results indicated that there is a relationship between professional preferences (dislikes), the stimulatory features of rejected professions, and emotional reactivity of the surveyed students. Perhaps temperament has a greater impact on the reluctance to perform certain professions than their positive selection (Paszkowska-Rogacz, 2011).

Another relevant issue is, to what extent the relationship between occupational activity and temperament changes under the influence of the work environment (Eliasz, 1981). Results of related studies involving people with long professional experience do not permit us to answer the question as to whether persons chose their occupation or occupational activities in correspondence with their temperament, or long-term performance of activities with specific occupational characteristics consequently leads to changes in temperament (Strelau, 2006).

The research conducted on temperament and empirical results cited above may undermine the predictive value of some questionnaires applied in occupational guidance in Ecuador, *Inventario Tipologico Temperamental* [Temperamental Typological Inventory] (author: Bastidas, 2003; revised by Davila Acosta) as the relation between occupational preferences and temperamental features of young person is problematic according to the empirical results.

To sum up, the relation between temperament and occupational preferences of young people, and effective performance in a specific work environment requires more research to support and explain possible relations between these variables.

2.3. Ability as an occupational success predictor

The concept 'ability' denotes the quality of a person being able to accomplish something with their physical or psychological resources. It stands for the individual's capacity to act physically or mentally. One of the most typical and adequate context of expression one's abilities is the workplace.

Among many factors of the complex decision-making process related to the career of young people is the domain of abilities that characterize an individual's potential and features to be actualized in the future work and coincides with person's competence in a specific occupation because of one's skill, training, or other qualification. Hence, one of the most crucial aspects to be considered in professional career planning is the valid and reliable diagnosis or identification of personal abilities. Among the different perspectives on abilities we may name the 3-factorial model of abilities that may affect career decisions and their outcomes (Gati, Fishman-Nadav, & Shiloh, 2006):

1. *How it is:* Objective abilities that condition possibilities of performing the selected career paths according to one's preferences, associated with intelligence;

2. *How I see it:* Assessment of one's own abilities;

3. *How I plan to use it:* Individual preferences and readiness to use a variety of one's own abilities in their future career, which directly shape career options that are considered as 'promising'.

The first of the above aspects is directly associated with human behavior in different task situations. In such situations the individual manifests a variety of specific physical and mental processes, such as speed and efficiency of thinking, creation of original ideas, eye-hand coordination, linguistic, artistic and mathematical skills, and technical abilities.

Differences that one may encounter between individuals are explained by such concepts as abilities, intelligence, special skills, talent, genius, mastery. Among these concepts the most distinguished are the general abilities correlated with intelligence and special skills. Intellectual activity has a distinguished position among many abilities important in vocational guidance. The best-known theories of intelligence are divided into structural (factorial), biological and cognitive theories. Intelligence may be defined as the global capacity of the individual to act purposefully and effectively in a rational way with his environment (Wechsler, 1944, as cited in Nęcka, 2004, pp. 758–759). Nęcka defines it as 'the ability to adapt to the circumstances on the basis of abstract relations, the individual's ability to notice, the use of prior experience and effective control over one's own cognitive processes' or Sternberg it defines simply as a goal-directed adaptive behavior (Sternberg, 2001, Sternberg, & Salter 1982). Special abilities according to Hornowski (1978) are in fact the sets of abilities that condition the level of performance of certain types of activities.

Some structural theories assume a hierarchy of skills, while others assume the existence of independent abilities. The creator of the first factor theories is Spearman who stated that all types of intellectual activity correspond to one fundamental function, and all remaining elements of intellectual activity appear in every case to be completely specific and different from the others (Spearman, 1904). It assumes the existence of a general factor g – general intelligence, which is involved in all types of intellectual activity, and s factors (specific). These factors are called special abilities and they require the participation of specific functions to perform specific tasks. Performance of a particular activity requires both the use of general factor g, which is common to all tasks, and the corresponding specific s factors in diversified intensity of activation of these factors.

A representative of this perspective is Vernon (1979), who identified two additional factors, verbal-school and spatial-manual, in addition to the main g-factor. These two factors are divided into smaller sub-groups and a much larger number of specific factors.

In contrast, the model presented by Catell and Horn (Catell, 1971) split the factor g into fluid intelligence gf, defined as the ability to perceive the relationship between symbols and perform operations on them and crystallized intelligence gc – which refers to the knowledge acquired and skills important in the specific socio-cultural context. The factor gf decreases with age, while the gc factor increases in importance in the course of intellectual development[25]. Apart from these taxonomies, 'second-order' factors were also identified, such as: the imagination, general cognitive fluency and overall cognitive speed.

Models of equivalent factors are an alternative to hierarchical factor models. They assume the existence of a number of equally important intellectual capacities. Thurstone (1938, as cited in Nęcka, 2003) conducted a factor analysis and distinguished independent factors related to mental abilities. These were: understanding of verbal information, verbal fluency, numerical abilities, memory abilities, speed of perception and object recognition, inductive reasoning and spatial visualization.

---

[25] Vernon (1979) states that intelligence is the product of the interplay between genetic potentiality and environmental stimulation.

As intelligence is directly rooted in the functioning of the brain, it also comprises such factors as neuronal transmission velocity, the efficiency of the nervous system and brain size. Behavioral, psycho-physiological and neuro-physiological studies confirm the relationship between intelligence and the speed of transmission of nervous system impulses, investigated in the research of Hobbes, Jensen, Vernon (as cited in Suświłło, 2004). Another important factor in brain efficiency is resistance to interference factors that meaningfully increase the level of competence in difficult tasks.

The above approaches: structural, biological and cognitive may belong to the psychometric approach, as they allow for intelligence to be measured. There is also a group of abilities that exceeds the classical IQ perspective and these refer to: social intelligence, moral, cultural, emotional, practical, and the theory of multiple intelligences. Among these theoretical approaches, social intelligence has the longest history of research. Thorndike defined it as the ability to understand people and behave adequately behavior toward other people (as cited in Grieve, & Mahar, 2013). Emotional intelligence refers to the ability of processing of information related to emotions. The most complete theory of that kind is considered the theory of Mayer and Salovey (1997) who distinguished four groups of abilities: 1) perceiving and expressing emotions, 2) including emotions in the process of thinking, 3) understanding and analyzing emotions and 4) managing emotions.

Practical intelligence is expressed in the ability to solve specific problems embedded in a certain context. Among the theories of practical intelligence, one worthy of special attention is the theory of tacit knowledge, which is (1) acquired in a self-study process (apart from school education and academic activity) (2) procedural knowledge and (3) practical knowledge applicable in a concrete situation.

Other approaches include multiple intelligence theory (IW) of Gardner (2002; see also Gardner, Kornhaber, & Wake, 2001) and Sternberg's theory of triarchic intelligence (Sternberg 2001; Sternberg, & Salter 1982). According to Gardner, 'intelligence' is a set of abilities that is somewhat independent of the other capacities of an individual, and comprises a basic set of operations for the processing of information. Gardner (2002) suggests the existence of at least seven strategies of perception and understanding the world that he treats as separate intelligences. An individual may apply specific skills related to each intelligence type to face and solve real problems related to the specific vocational activity.

The seven types of intelligence according to Gardner are:

1. Verbal-Linguistic – the ability to use words and language;

2. Logical-Mathematical – the ability to conduct inductive and deductive reasoning, the use of numbers and recognition of abstract patterns;

3. Visual-Spatial (also as musical intelligence) – the ability to visualize objects and spatial dimensions and imaginary skills;

4. Physical-Motor (kinesthetic intelligence) – body capacity and the ability to control body movements;

5. Environmental and Nature – the ability to distinguish, classify and correctly identify and apply the properties of the natural environment;

6. Interpersonal – the ability to communicate and create adequate human relationships;

7. Intrapersonal (also as existential intelligence) – the ability to identify, distinguish feelings and create mental models of self.

In line with the author's theory, each person represents a different system of capabilities which are unique to the human species. Each of these abilities has their own different locations in the areas of the brain, and can be developed through appropriate training and education. In the context of the theory of multiple intelligences one should mention the concept of moral intelligence (Lennick, & Kiel, 2007) – which refers to the ability to adequately distinguish between behaviors that develop the person from behavior that damages the individual or others.

Psychologists involved in counseling have always expressed the preference for multi-dimensional concepts of intelligence (Guichard, & Huteau, 2005). The advantage of applying such complex concepts of cognitive abilities is that they permit the association of the various forms of intelligence with different sets of work activity. An individual choosing the specific profession is usually guided towards occupations corresponding to their predispositions and skills, which allow them to be successful in some specific abilities.

These abilities usually correspond to different forms of intelligence. For example, Gardner (2002) illustrates the different types of intelligence by presenting the corresponding activities: the poet – when dealing with linguistic intelligence; sailor, engineer, surgeon, sculptor – referring to spatial intelligence; dancer, athlete, craftsman – when dealing with physical (kinesthetic) intelligence; salespeople, politicians, teachers are directly related to interpersonal intelligence. It is questionable if one may use only these types of intelligence in the case of abilities related to the existing classification of occupations.

It seems the concept of abilities conditioning efficient performance at a concrete job may be more complex than the perspective of ability as intelligence alone can provide. On the one hand, professions may not be simply and distinctly classified into in clear categories of abilities. On the other, many occupations of a similar nature require different abilities.

Borman, Hanson and Hedge (1997) argue that the person–job fit selection process should consider ability level. Though intellectual ability may only approximately predict performance in an occupational group, abilities are one of the best predictors of efficiency in the specific group. In other words, the results of intelligence is a good predictor of success at work, even if occupations are characterized by a very complex set of abilities necessary for success. Moreover, as demonstrated in the study of Judge, Klinger and Simon (2010), even people who perform simple work earn more and are more successful if endowed with high intelligence than workers in the same position with lower intelligence.

The models presented usually assume the possibility of objective/adequate measurement of intelligence via the psychological assessment of an individual. However, apart from the objective intelligence assessment results, it is important to include a subjective assessment of the individual's skills and abilities.

Abilities that are related to self-assessment (*How do I see myself?*) directly reflect an individual's belief in their own competence (Bandura, 2001). The measurement of both objective competence and self-perception of competences is an important issue in occupational counseling. Prediger (2004) emphasized the importance of this information, as this knowledge is obtained for long period of time through experience in the form of information from family, friends and employers. Assessment of capabilities understood as a predisposition to do something, to perform better than others at certain tasks or activities may deeply influence the choice of a profession and better predict professional satisfaction and success than results of tests of ability and intelligence (Hornowski, 1978; Prediger, 1999). Individual very often trust their own feelings and beliefs much more than test results that position their specific skills and abilities in a ranking.

One of theories based on the self-knowledge of the candidate to choose an occupation on the basis of assessment of own abilities is Prediger's (1999) classification scheme, which distinguishes 15 types of capabilities associated with the practice:

1. READING – reading and understanding;
2. COUNTING – making correct mathematical calculations; applied mathematics;
3. LANGUAGE UNDERSTANDING – identifying the correct and incorrect use of language;
4. HELPING OTHERS – nursing or teaching; assistance in making decisions, solving problems;
5. CONTACTING PEOPLE – speaking; making a good impression; having good relations with others;
6. SALE – persuading to buy a particular product, service;
7. LEADERSHIP/MANAGEMENT – directing/managing people in order to work for the common good;
8. ORGANIZATION – attention to detail; control and systematic execution of tasks;
9. WORKING IN THE OFFICE – quick and accurate performance of tasks such as information retrieval, sorting, recording expenses, keeping an address book;
10. MANUAL SKILLS – creation and repair of everyday objects;
11. SCIENTIFIC SKILLS – understanding the laws of physics in everyday life, the knowledge of simple machines;
12. SPATIAL VISION – observing and drawing objects and imagining how they would look like from different angles;
13. ACADEMIC – understanding the laws governing the world, scientific work;
14. ARTISTIC ABILITIES – drawing, painting, playing instruments, acting, dancing and so on;
15. LITERARY SKILLS – expressing ideas or feelings in writing.

This classification system served during the stage of identifying the predictive validity of the IPPJ questionnaire, and so it will be discussed in the description of the design of the IPPJ diagnostic tool.

So far we have discussed categorizing capabilities and conducting a self-assessment of them. A third aspect of the issue is personal preferences or interests that determine the willingness of individuals to use different skills in their future careers. According to Tyszkowa (1990), interests help individuals to develop abilities when they are related to individual preferences.

2.4. Interests as personality traits

Occupational interests are key factors in the psychology of individual differences and in career intervention contexts as they are associated with vocational-relevant variables such as abilities, success, and satisfaction. From the very beginning of the development in the area of vocational guidance, personality was considered a direct expression of vocational interests, and both interests and personality were supposed to share a analogous structure (Holland, 1985, Rossier, 2015). Though there is a positive correlation between interests and satisfaction, the empirical data don't confirm the direct relationship between interests and actual relevant abilities and related performance. According to Barak and Rabi (1981) relation between abilities and interests is mediated by cognitive factors such as perceived abilities, expected success, and anticipated satisfaction.

Vocational interests are rather socio-culturally specific factors, influenced rather by shared environments and life experience-dependent variables (Betsworth, Bouchard, Cooper, Grotevant, Hansen, & Scarr, 1994) than the biological and genetic factors of career. At a more social level, sharing common interests enables people to build a network of people who enjoy facing the specific challenges of work life and enjoy performing their own, often monotonous occupation without boredom for many years.

It is quite obvious that people representing different occupational realities are, or at least should be, differentiated by specific interests. While speaking with a lawyer, doctor, teacher, dancer or psychologist we immediately discover distinct topics of their conversations, work concerns and differing reasons for their personal successes and professional challenges.

Many attempts have been made to define what interests are, and what their meaning is and how they function in the development of an individual's vocational career. According to Lowman and Carson (2003, p. 478): 'Interests are relatively stable psychological characteristics of people which identify the personal evaluation (subjective attributions of 'goodness' or 'badness') related to the specific occupational or leisure activity area'.

Two main perspectives on the concept of interest may be identified in theoretical approaches. The first is the contextual approach, represented, for example, by Schraw and Lehman (2001). They relate interest with the performance of a specific type of activities, which as a result generates the experience of positive emotions in contact with certain types of objects or actions. Hence, vocational interests are generally developed when an individual follows their personal preferences and positive emotions, performing some jobs and naturally avoiding other activities. Gurycka's definition of interest (1978, pp. 33–34) presents a similar position, where interest is a 'relatively stable, observable tendency to explore the surrounding world, it has a form of directed/ defined cognitive activity of a specific intensity and is manifested in a selective attitude to the surrounding reality'.

The second approach treats interest as dispositions, or persistent, permanent human tendencies to favor activity associated with a particular type of objects or classes of objects through selectivity (Campbell, 1971; Gurycka, 1978; Matczak, 1991; Schiefele, Krapp, & Winteler, 1992; Strong, 1943).

Selectivity mentioned in this definition means that a person perceives some features of the objects and relationships between them. In such situations the individual tends to investigate them and to experience specific feelings (positive and negative) related to the whole process. When the attitude accompanying the activity is characterized by primarily emotional involvement, it is expressed by intensive attention and focus on something. Long-term interest in a certain vocational field enables an individual to develop necessary expert knowledge and mastery skills and greatly facilitates the process of acquiring a proficiency in activities performed. Interest increases attention and focus on something. Summing up, interests: (1) are relatively stable over time, but are influenced by the environment; (2) have an impact on behavior by inducing motivation; (3) reflect the identity of the individual.

According to Super's (1972) perspective on the mechanism of interest development and functioning, there are three interesting assumptions: (1) there is no essential difference between aptitude and interest; (2) interests are a trait of character or personality; (3) interest has a distinct nature and cannot be reduced to abilities, nature nor personality traits.

As the phenomenon of human interests is apparently difficult to grasp, Super (1984) proposed four methods of diagnosis in reference to his operational definitions of interests. The first one is to answer the questions: 'What do you like to do?' and 'What professions are you interested in?' Some people answer such questions: 'Nothing is interesting to me; I do not know what interests me'. Such responses are usually due to the lack of introspection skills and very limited self-knowledge. Sometimes the difficulty to grasp and express one's own interests is in line with the belief that interests refer only to a spectacular passion or hobby. This category of people is simply ashamed to admit that their passions are long talks via internet, skype, facebook, tweeter or computer games.

The second method to research interests relies on the daily observation of somebody's or one's own activities (Super, 1984). It is rather obvious that all activities undertaken freely by people reflect their authentic preferences and real commitment. To the contrary, if the person is quickly discouraged and easily abandons certain actions, it is a sign of a lack of that specific interest.

Third, psychologists use attention, memory and knowledge tests in the study of interests (Super, 1984). The more a person is interested, the more they will seek specific information that is attractive to them; very often that happens without them noticing it, in an unconscious process of remembering without any effort, just because it is interesting. Finally, the individual realizes how much they know about some specific topics that are also related to certain occupational profiles. The humorous definition of the best professional career is: 'Find the job that is your hobby and let people pay you for it.' In vocational counseling practice one may encounter a set of methods and interest inventories (Harrington, & Long, 2013). They are to support practitioners as they work to find out client interests, skills, motivations, and other personal traits that help youth self-define and construct their career path.

These are professionally-developed psychological tools, and their diagnostic results are compared with the results of people performing certain professions. Psychometric tools may be useful in the diagnosis of interests, because the profile of interests may be clearly related and fit into specific vocational classifications.

To sum up, interests play an important role in most contemporary theories of career development (Guichard, & Huteau, 2005; Holland, 1997; Lent, Brown, & Hacket, 1994, Super, 1980). The interest and preferences diagnosis enables individuals to increase their self-awareness, identify with possible career options and stimulate their search for an adequate professional path. It is vocational interests which largely condition and determine career choice, are the key concept in the person-work environment fit as well as an indicator of the general well-being of the individual (Meir, 1989).

The theory of vocational interests emerges from the assumptions of the theory of traits and factor theories, and as such interests are treated as personal dispositions. The most frequently-used categorization guiding the exploration of occupational interests is Holland's (1997) theory of vocational personality types and work environment. This perspective on professional guidance will be basis for the methodology of occupational preferences and the questionnaire for the diagnosis, which will be presented in more detail in the next chapters.

2.5. Beliefs and values as vocational preferences predictors

Values are considered to be the fundamental guiding force for human behavior. What are values? How are values understood? Despite the large number and diversity of many characteristics of values, generally they are an interplay of mental processes with a combination of cognitive representations such as concepts, goals, with emotional components characterized by positive or negative valence.

Both cognitive and emotional traits in values associated with career are composed of some mental concepts of job or self-concept of a being a good physician or forester accompanied by some emotional attitudes that view one's career as positive (satisfactory and successful occupation) or negative (boring and exhausting job).

Values may be expressed in both: the pursuit of something, such as money, power, spirituality or the opposite, as the avoidance of some tangible and intangible assets (Misamichi, 1998). Therefore values function and indicate criteria for many human choices.

Values have the nature of judgments about how important something is to us. Values may be defined operationally as individual's beliefs that indicate how he or she thinks that things are or ought to be (Fairholm, 2013). However, at the very beginning of any attempt to grasp the core of values and their relation to beliefs one should mention that people often do not behave according to their beliefs, even their expressed ones. Beliefs as such are only weakly related and predictive of actual future behavior. There is the distinction between what is desired in real behavior and what is expressed in somebody's beliefs. This difference coincides with how people behave in reality and what people say they value (Misamichi, 1998).

Thus a valuable distinction to be considered in vocational counseling concerns values as what people actually desire, as opposed to what they think ought to be desired because of the influence of common trends or fashion, parents or colleagues choices. The relation described is also about beliefs, and refers to 'how it should be' and 'how it is in fact,' namely, how people behave. This may be expressed in such situations as one's career, especially in the kind of work that individuals may choose freely, not only when they perform a job according to more or less conscious and personal beliefs.

The concept of values has long been the subject of psychological research, including Rokeach (as cited in Brown, & Brooks, 1984), Allport, Vernon, Lindzey (as cited in Brzozowski, 2007), and Schwartz and Bilsky (1990), who created the theory of basic human values, understood as latent motivations and needs. Some scholars identify values with interests, while other researchers tend to relate them with needs. Super and Bohn (1971) propose the following definition: values are the targets (objects) that are necessary to satisfy a need. In that context interests are specific, concrete actions that emerge from values and are the road to needs satisfaction.

The study of an individual's values enables us to understand how people work and why they decide to do something. While the study of interests enables some specific educational and professional behavior to be predicted, an individual's value system may give more insight into the underlying aspects of why they do what they do, why they work where they work. One specific value may lead to not just one but several different types of activities that serve to satisfy a specific need.

It is important to mention that values refer to what is desirable while confronting the process of specific needs satisfaction. Usually, values do not work alone as distinct entities in the human mind; they create a complex flux that underlies a personal value system. One might assume that each value system has a hierarchic structure, which results in assigning a different ranking according to the importance and priority of specific values. A system of values is not a constant permanent state, however, and it is subject to such factors as age, education, culture and personal experience. A general classification of values exists; however, there is no universal list of values. Despite many taxonomies of values, employment is listed very high in the axiological ranking characteristic to contemporary civilization.

The aim of the study coordinated by Nevill and Super (1986) was to develop techniques that permit the study of the following 21 work-related values such as: (1) development of one's abilities, (2) achievement of mastery, (3) physical effort, (4) promotion, (5) aesthetics (beauty), (6) altruism (helping others), (7) authority (including management), (8) autonomy (independence), (9) creativity, (10) material benefits (high standard, comfort), (11) life-style (work-life balance), (12) self-development, (13) physical activity, (14) prestige (admiration, respect), (15) risk (challenge), (16) social interactions (action in the group), (17) social relations (colleagues, friends), (18) variability (diversity), (19) friendly work environment, (20) sharing experiences and worldview, (21) certainty and economic security.

As a result of the international project entitled: Work Importance Study (Super, & Nevill, 1984) a method enabling cross-cultural study of motivation to work concerning different social roles was conducted, including an analysis of work commitment and life career and their relationship with the subjective quality of life. The WIS technique is used in career counseling in many European countries to provide knowledge about individuals. It may be integrated into the counseling process for people planning their careers.

Evaluation of the personal hierarchy of values is an integral part of a strategy to determine life choices, develop the self-awareness of the individual and as such is particularly useful in the formation of motivation to work and career guidance. Schein (2006) came to this conclusion on the basis of empirical research that demonstrated there is a close relationship between the preferred system of values, needs, and the preferred set of competences. Schein distinguished eight career groups according to such values, metaphorically labeling them career 'anchors'. Though there are eight career themes, Schein (2006) states that people usually identify themselves with one or two anchors. Each of the anchors is represented by the following competencies:

1. **Professional Competence**. Accompanied by the need to 'be an expert' in a particular field, professional competence aims to confirm one's own precedence in occupational expertise. People with such a value system are usually not interested in managerial positions; they are usually placed in some technical or functional areas where they apply and continue to develop those skills. This type of person derives their sense of identity from the exercise of their own skills integrated with their technical or functional professional competence.

2. **Managerial Competence**. The main professional goal in this area is acquiring new experience in management and decision-making, increasing one's range of authority and pursuing financial success. It is usually necessary in a horizontal managerial position shift, in contrary to the first anchor. This type of person seeks to climb to a higher level of organization to challenge and integrate their skills and efforts and fulfill their ambition to be a main manager as soon as possible.

3. **Autonomy and independence**. This competency is associated with efforts to broaden one's own freedom, release upsetting ties and restrictions (e.g. related to autocratic bureaucracy and superiors). People strongly oriented

towards independence do not necessarily seek leadership positions, at the same time; they do not want to carry out the commands of their superiors. Their goal is to work as independent professionals with related responsibilities.

4. **Security and stabilization.** The main driving force in this case is an emotional relationship with the company and a sense of loyalty. Such employees have a strong need for security and if they aspire to leadership positions, it is mostly in the same organizational unit. This category of person seeks the opportunity to define work in their own way. They usually defend themselves against changes in their organizational environment; for example, they are not interested in an international career.

5. **Entrepreneurial creativity**. This anchor theme manifests itself in the fact that creative people seek to have knowledge about themselves, the organization and its various subsystems. They see problems and try to solve them by changes and innovation, etc. They are usually mobile and positive about rotation as a way to develop skills and attain horizontal professional promotion. Such persons tend to take risks to overcome possible obstacles. One of the varieties of creativity is entrepreneurship.

6. **Services and dedication to others**. For this type of personality, the main purpose in life becomes realization of humanistic values, solving political problems, helping others, medical treatment, teaching, solving environmental problems, developing social harmony and inclusion, improving people's safety, curing diseases. People with these values willingly engage in social activities and/or take a job as a volunteer.

7. **Challenge**. The underlying motivator of action here is often a desire to overcome difficulty and take risks. Individuals who enjoy challenge are willing to take a job in an environment which creates the opportunity to fight and compete. Challenge-type people look for solutions to apparently unsolvable problems; they tend to prevail in spite of serious opposition and overcome problems and limitations. Pure challenge is the motivation of their activity; e.g., the engineer who is generally interested in creating an impossibly difficult design. Possible challenges can range widely, from saving a company from bankruptcy to trade and sports.

8. **Life style**. People representing this value try to preserve the work-life balance and harmony between various aspects of life, above all, their job and personal life. They are ready to give up higher incomes to spend more time with loved ones. Success for them is more than professional success; that is why such people look for a career situation that will have enough flexibility to achieve such work-life integration.

Schein (2006) presents a career as a cone shape. First, he distinguishes the objective progression of a career, defined by the environment and subjective evaluation, based on the employee's own aspirations. Second, each career shift may run in a horizontal plane, a vertical one or 'in depth' of an organization. A person who gains satisfaction in climbing up the ladder of an organization will be satisfied in professions and jobs with organizational hierarchy, such as the military. Horizontal career shifts assume constant development of a specific competence, allowing individuals to change positions and areas of responsibilities in the range of one hierarchical level of the organization. The third option – a career shift 'in depth' of the organization occurs when the indicator of success is gaining power and influence, resulting from many years of work in the same company. Examples of this shift often refer to the job position of a secretary or porters.

Schein's (2006) concept of the 'career anchor' is a conceptual advance in assessing career orientations that states that a young person starts their career with certain ambitions, doubts, expectations but also false impressions and through their work experiences discovers real interests, values and real skills required in the work. These experiences contribute a lot and are necessary to shape gradually the career identity and the self-concept that becomes his/her career anchor.

The advantage of *anchors theory* is that people may recognize their preferences for specific areas typical for their job. Persons that follow and fulfill specific professional roles in their career path satisfy their specific needs and follow values typical for their career anchors.

2.6. Personality and vocation

Another factor that may serve to diagnose and predict the future career profile of a young person is personality; and more specifically, the professional personality. School counselors attempt to help students in career development by considering their specific personality traits so they achieve success in school, at work and are ready to self-fulfillment as responsible members of society.

In many cultures – especially individualistic ones, when somebody wants to learn who we are, we are rather asked 'What do you do?' Acquiring vocational identity may be seen as an important factor in shaping personality. That is, finding a profession that may express our personality best.

What is personality? In short, personality is typically considered the sum of all the behavioral and mental characteristics that make the individual unique in patterns of thinking, feeling and behaving (Kazdin, 2000). The study of personality focus on two broad areas: One understands individual differences in particular personality characteristics, such as sociability or irritability. The other explains how the various parts of a person come together as a whole.

The idea of personality typology for the use of psychology appeared first with the works of Jung (1921) who indicated the central dimensions of personality described on the continuum Introversion-extraversion. It was developed in publications that appeared in 1938 by Darley and Guilford, Christensen, Bond and Sutton (as cited in Holland, 1997). Darley suggested that vocational knowledge may result in determination of a professional stereotype; in turn, Guilford and colleagues distinguished six factors shaping professional interests into the following categories: mechanical, scientific, social care, clerical, enterprising and aesthetic.

This chapter on the role of personality in vocational guidance presents the theoretical basis for the construction of the questionnaire based on the concept of the Holland's (1997) theory of vocational personality. Much research has attempted to examine the convergence of personality and professional preferences (Holland, 1985, 1997). Holland confirmed that vocational interests are directly related to personality. Though some research has shown that an individual's occupational interests significantly change over time, Holland explained that it was a result of an incomplete process of crystallization and clarification reflected in inconsistent and undifferentiated profiles (Holland 1997).

At this point it is worth mentioning other psychological theories of human types such as Eysenck's (1976) three-factors model, Cattell's (1957) model of 16 personality traits reconstructed on the basis of factor analysis or one of the most widely used, the Minnesota Multiphasic Personality Inventory (MMPI), with its latest version, the MMPI-2-RF, revised in 2008. Another theoretical and psychometric strategy of personality measurement related to the concept of career-person fit was created by two American authors: Myers and Briggs (as cited in Tieger, Barron-Tieger, 1999). They used the theoretical assumptions of Jung's theory, expanding them and developing its applicative aspects, constructing a questionnaire for the diagnosis of human types known in as Myers-Briggs Type Indicator or in short (MBTI). The questionnaire is designed to help people realize their 'best fit type'. This description of personality uses types based on four basic aspects:

• **Extraversion or Introversion**: the way in which people enter into relationships with the world, how and what stimulates them most: extraversion vs. introversion. This type refers to how the person manages his/her attention and energy, whether she/he focuses on people and things in the outer world, or on her/him inner world;

• **Sensing or Intuition**: This type is defined by the individual's way of perceiving and dealing with information: whether they focus on basic information or tend to interpret it and add their own meaning;

• **Thinking or Feeling**: the way in which people draw conclusions and make decisions. This personality refers to typical decision-making strategies. It may be objective and logical, or subjective;

• **Judging or Perceiving**: this refers to the attitude of people in the world, whether they tend to make decisions or continuously stay open to new information.

The authors of MBTI established eight personality types, which are described in four bipolar scales, according to the dimensions above. If we consider one indicator for each scale the person filling the questionnaire will receive their personality profile identified according to the four dichotomies. They form a combination of four scales defined in the MBTI personality typology. Possible combinations result in a total of 16 personality types. Each type specifies the following aspects: the general purpose of the individual's life, learning styles, educational path, and appropriate profession and the way in which a person arrange relations with people.

A short description of individuals with these specific preferences is presented in Tables 4. Each identified characteristic by an acronym.

Table 4a. Indicators of personality types of the Myers-Briggs

Preferences concerning the stimulation source	
Extraversion/Introversion (E/I)	
Extraversion (E)	**Introversion (I)**
• obtains energy from the outside world • focused on humans or things • active • broad interests • experience precedes understanding • interaction • seeks to meet people • gets energy spending time with people	• obtains energy from the inner world • focuses on thoughts, concepts • reflective, thought "oriented" • deep interest • understanding precedes experience • concentration • introspective orientation • get energy spending time alone

Source: Tieger, Barron-Tieger 1999.

Table 4b. Indicators of personality types of the Myers-Briggs

Perception preferences			
The way of taking decisions (T/F)		**The way of taking in information (S/N)**	
Thinking (T)	**Feeling (F)**	**Sensing (S)**	**Intuition (N)**
• analysis • objectivity • logic • criticism	• sympathies • subjectivism • sensitivity • personal approach	• realism • pragmatism • accuracy • sequential process-ing of information	• innovation • variability • fantasy • foreboding trusting

Source: Tieger, Barron-Tieger 1999.

Table 4c. Indicators of personality types of the Myers-Briggs

Relation to the outer world (J/P)	
Judging (J)	**Perceiving (P)**
• organization • stabilization • planning • determination • striving for aims • systematic	• improvisation • flexibility • spontaneity • trying to observe • follows the course of events • openness to change

Source: Tieger, Barron-Tieger, 1999.

The five-factor model by Costa McCrae (1992) is a representation of personality structure that has become recently one of the most widespread models of personality. The five factors: Openness, Conscientiousness, Extraversion, Agreeableness and Neuroticism (OCEAN) are measures used to study the most discriminative personality traits.

Openness to experience is typical for inventive, curious, creative and imaginative persons that tend to avoid routine and appreciate variety with diversity of experience such as adventures, art, unconventional and novel ideas. Persons with high openness to experience are more inclined to self-actualization, while persons with low openness are rather pragmatic with their feet on the ground.

Conscientiousness characterizes persons that are very efficient, careful, task-oriented and well-organized with high self-discipline. They have a preference to planned activity rather than spontaneous behavior. Persons with low conscientiousness are more flexible and spontaneous, and can be perceived and unreliable.

Extraversion is usually expressed in an energetic, outgoing style of living. This type of people look for stimulation, are usually more talk-active and sociable. High extraversion is frequently associated with tendency to be dominant and attention-seeking, while low extraversion denotes reserved persons with a more reflective personality.

Agreeableness denotes usually friendly, cooperative and sympathetic persons that are more trustful and helpful than others. This sort of people may be considered naive or submissive in their agreeableness and avoidance of direct confrontation with others.

Neuroticism characterizes sensitive, less emotionally stable and unsecure persons with higher level of anxiety. For their sensitivity they easily become angry, upset and more vulnerable in social relations. High neuroticism describes very dynamic persons that may be perceived as rather unbalanced. People with lower neuroticism are usually more stable and calm, but can be seen as individuals without any passion and bored.

The *Big Five* Personality dimensions model was one of the most commonly used to see the convergence of Costa McCrae's OCEAN and Holland's vocational personality dimensions: Realistic, Investigative, Artistic, Social, Entrepreneurial, Conventional, commonly abbreviated with the acronym RIASEC. The study confirmed the coherence of two models (Costa, McCrae & Holland 1984) which fully confirmed Holland's conviction that occupational interests are an expression of personality. The most consistent relationships appeared between Extraversion and two RIASEC dimensions, namely: Social and Enterprising types; between Openness and both Artistic and Investigative RIASEC interests; and between Agreeableness and the Social RIASEC type.

Barrick, Mount and Gupta (2003) has consistently shown that three of the six Holland orientations are represented within the Five Factor Model of Personality: Artistic correlates with Openness, Social with Openness and Agreeableness, and Enterprising correlates with Extraversion. A large sample analysis (N = 70.000) by Peassler (2015) evidences the higher male variability in cognitive abilities and physical attributes that resulted in is significantly higher vocational interests change among man. The results also confirmed that while men varied more in Realistic and Enterprising interests, women varied more in Artistic and Conventional interests.

These variability differences impact on the female–male ratios in vocational interests noticeable in gender disparities in particular fields of work and education disciplines. Additionally empirical studies revealed that gender differences in variability weaken with age (Peassler, 2015; Yang, & Barth, 2015).

While personality type does not determine future career success, it may meaningfully help to discover what motivates people most to act, and in consequence may support and enable selection of the appropriate profession, in accordance with the described features. Generally, the more aspects of the employee's personality that are appropriate and fit the job, the greater the satisfaction and success at work. Additionally, in the early study of Linton in 1945 (as cited in Holland, 1997), he demonstrated a close relationship between cultural environment and the personalities of individuals living in the environment. This convinced Holland that one can explore specific characteristics of an environment by indicating characteristics of the personality of individuals functioning in a specific environment.

Holland's theory of personality[26] (1959, 1997) implies that it is possible to identify 6 personality types: Realistic, Investigative, Artistic, Social, Enterprising and Conventional. It is significant that RIASEC personality types obtained for individuals using Holland's questionnaire are correlated with descriptions or self-descriptions (Holland 1997) of these persons in the line with adjectives listed below (Figure 4).

Figure 4. Descriptions of persons with specific types (adapted from Holland, 1957, 1997)

---

[26] Described in detail in a separate chapter below.

It is significant that RIASEC personality types obtained for individuals using Holland's questionnaire correlated with descriptions or self-descriptions (Holland, 1997) of these persons.

Ott-Holland, Huang, Ryan, Elizondo, & Wadlington (2013) proved there are differences in following one's own professional interests and career choice across cultures and may be associated with gender differences in interests. In some cases societal and gender expectations may impact on free decision of youth concerning their individual personality and interests. The research by Barrick, Mount, and Gupta (2003) has shown cross-cultural variation in regard with the gender and vocational interests. Results indicated that high in-group collectivism (GLOBE dimension) that the link between personality traits and interests and vocational choices is weaker in contrast with less collectivistic societies. Moreover, it was evidenced that the gender egalitarianism (GLOBE model) influenced the level of gender differences in interests, surprisingly indicating that gender differences may be wider in egalitarian cultures. All these implications are valuable for vocational counseling in highly diverse, multicultural society of Ecuador.

2.7. Stages of career development

Career development is the continuous process of managing one's life, formal and informal education and work. The core of the theory of career choice is the assumption of the continuous life-long development of each person (Super 1984). This developmental perspective on the path of professional development has significantly contributed to the better understanding of mechanisms and rules guiding career choices of youth as well as adults.

Theories related to human development are a complementary contribution, as they help to explain existing models of maturation phases. Some of these theories focus on the concept of self-image and the concept of self-construction in the context of work and other related life roles (Savickas, & Lent, 1994). This perspective fits in the rich tradition of developmental psychology, which initially dealt largely with the period of childhood, but later also focused on the search and analysis of individual paths of development during the entire course of life (Brzezińska, 2000; Overton, 2010).

Human life falls outside any definitions, as it is usually a unique consequence of many unpredictable variables. In the psychological literature, we encounter different approaches and classifications of the human life cycle. Among many approaches, career-based perspectives may be encountered that provide valuable and essential information on the nature of occupational development (Super, 1957, 1980, 1984; Super, & Bohn, 1971).

Career development is closely related to human life phases and is a lifelong process. Career development is defined as the psychological and behavioral processes influenced by personal and contextual factors that shape one's career over the life span. Therefore, career growth involves the person's contribution of a career construction, decision-making style, and integration of life roles, values, and self concepts (Herr, & Cramer, 1996).

Personal development may be seen as a framework for career development. As psychologists discern distinct developmental phases and milestones, we may also propose some predictable schemes that underlie more universal models of career development. Career is a set of subsequent transitions shaped by the complex flux of personal factors such as: value system, career-life aspirations, specific way of perceiving different life experiences and so on (Herr, & Cramer, 1996). Indicating more common sequences of events and experiences regarding career phases is a valuable contribution, which enables career counselors to support and accompany young people in their career planning.

Educational institutions provide career counselors to support students with their career and educational development. Knowledge about the nature and dynamics of specific problems likely to occur in each of the career phases is a prerequisite for successful career design and 'navigation'. The impact of career development on young people is long-term and incalculable. Thus young people begin to shape or rather fashion their own work identity through the process of career development (Tiedeman, & O'Hara, 1963).

The theory of Ginzberg (1984) proposes that the developmental process leads to professional career formation in three stages: fantasy, tentative and realistic. The child accumulates different experiences that consolidate in future activities preferences. Once initiated in childhood, the development of the career profile continues in the preteen years and through high school, when the young person finally identifies their interests, competence and values typical for final occupational choice.

In the first fantasy stage (until 11 years), children perform typical role play, make pretend certain activities, and begin to figure out their own future careers. In this phase children usually make illogical and rather arbitrary choices that often do not match with their reality. In the second, tentative stage (11–17 years), individuals become more aware of their preferences (what they like, and what not), skills and needs. They more seriously consider real-life aspects that impact the range of their choices. Finally, in the realistic stage (17–24 years) youth express their internal decisions about concrete career paths (Ginzberg, 1984). The process of career development is clearly highlighted in the decision-making process, whereby career choices are made in a series of steps.

In line with Super (1980), an individual's self-concept changes over time and develops as an outcome of life experience. Young people successively refine and adapt their own self-concept over time and apply it to the world of work, which is expressed in the career choice. Super (1980) states that human development consists of five closely interrelated life and career development stages: childhood, adolescence, early adulthood, middle adulthood, and late adulthood (Paszkowska-Rogacz, 2011). Within these stages five phases of career development are observed.

While this model is based on the Western European countries' experience and empirical evidence, it might serve as a reference in the analysis and further investigation of the phases typical for youth in Ecuador.

The name of each phase determines its typical developmental task:

I. Growth phase – from birth to 14 years – the stage of childhood.

This developmental phase is marked by the individual identifying with some role models and important persons in the family and at school. The core process of this phase is the development of one's self-concept, attitudes, values system and preliminary idea of the world of work. In the beginning of this phase, the most important role is played by needs and fantasies about the future, then – with the increase of activity and participation of young people in society – the role of interests and skills increases. This phase includes three periods:

• **fantasy period** – from 4 to 10 years of age: the core of this period are the specific needs of the child and the performing of their first important social roles, initially as play-like activities;

• **interests period** – from 11 to 12 years old: during these two years "what one likes" becomes the main factor of personal aspiration and activity;

• **capacities period** – from 13 to 14 years old: this is a period of analysis of one's own abilities in the context of specific professional requirements.

II. Exploration phase – from 15 to 24 years old – the stage of adolescence.

A typical feature of this phase is testing different social roles and gaining professional experience during school, leisure and work time. This phase of preliminary crystallization of professional preference comprises 3 sub-periods:

• **tentative period** – from 15 to 17 years: characterized by making preliminary choices (often expressed in discussions, fantasies, work attempts). Typical choices are based on needs, interests, skills, values and available opportunities;

• **transition period** – from 18 to 21 years: this is a specification stage dominated by choices and activities contextualized by real possibilities related to entering the labor market or professional training;

• **trial period** – from 22 to 24 years: this is the time of defining the most possible area of professional activity; usually it is related to taking the first job and testing that specific job as one's own permanent professional activity.

III. Establishment phase – from 25 to 44 years of age; the stage of early adulthood.

The main effort in this stage is focused on finding permanent and secure employment, after the choice of the main field of employment on the basis of previous experiences and trials. This relates to occupations requiring specialized training as well as occupations where no specific training was necessary. Typical stages of this phase are:

• **trial period** – from 25 to 30 years; the selected occupation may be disappointing, which usually leads to job changes and new decisions until the final occupation is defined. Another option in this phase may be recognition and acceptance of the lack of skills and competences necessary for successful performance of a particular type of work;

• **stabilization period** – from 31 to 44 years; typical of this phase is that the career profile is clearly outlined and defined. Characteristic efforts and ventures focus on implementing the clarified career model. For many people, this period is the most creative time in career development.

IV. Maintenance phase – from 45 to 64 years of age – a stage of professional maturity.

The main effort of in this phase is the stabilization of activities undertaken in the chosen career path. A typical task of the consolidation phase is developing previous activities rather than initiating new ones.

V. Decline phase – from 65 years – senior age stage and readiness for retirement.

The Decline phase is characterized by the significant decrease or disappearance of typical professional activities. A significant restriction is imposed by increasing health problems and limitation of physical and mental capabilities. Individuals may also initiate new areas of activity. While initially this may be in the form of partial participation, afterward this activity is limited to an observer role. Elementary phases of this period are:

• **disengagement period** – from 65 to 70 years: this is usually a period of official retirement, and infrequently it may take the form of an increasing reduction of the previous range of work duties. Another marker of this phase is the limitation of scope of activities according to the factual efficiency of the human body. Some people also seek part-time work;

• **retirement period** – over 71 years: generally this is the termination of any professional activity, however there are strong individual differences; namely some agree to completely depart from career-related activities with acceptance of that new mode of functioning as a retired person, while others do not agree to leave their previous style of life and activities related to the job performed. This may result in the lack of acceptance of role reversal.

Another important theoretical trend in professional guidance is the social cognitive view of career development and counseling created by Lent and Brown. It focuses on cognitive processes and variables that shape career behavior and view people as active actors and decision makers in their career development (Brown, 2002). Social Cognitive Career Theory (SCCT) is a quite recent concept that firstly aims to combine the valuable contributions of such researchers as Super, Holland, and Bandura, and secondly, to highlight the importance of personal and sociostructural aspects in development of vocational interests, occupational choices and factors that impact the level of career success and steadiness (as cited in Lent, & Brown, 2005).

According to the educational system and the crucial period for the decision of vocational path in Ecuador, it has been determined[27] that the self-consciousness of the preferences of youth seems to have its key moment after completing the second, 4-year stage of secondary education (college) at the age of 17–18 years.

---

[27] As it is a moment of the major of studies and the University choice.

At this stage the student is obliged to decide about their future education profile and career preferences. Decisions made in that key moment of life have a direct impact on future professional activity, work performance and life satisfaction.

The knowledge and understanding of the stages of human career development allows for the definition of typical needs and challenges of the individual in their career. It enables us to specify the specific psychosocial profile of youth (16–19 years) that took part in the research project aiming to create the Ecuadorian version of the questionnaire. Developmental theories allow us to determine the specific point of the student's life at certain level of education to better support youth in the decision making process in effective cooperation with a professional counselor.

Summing up, on the basis of general models of career development, and the analysis of the course of education, as a space for the most critical exploration and crystallization, it is possible to indicate the critical moments when the vocational counseling is necessary for the most adequate intervention and help in career choices.

2.8. Career decisions of youth

In the literature on professional guidance, the issue of vocational choice has recently been gaining research interest. Career choice may be regarded as one of the most important life decisions individuals have to make (Nauta, & Kahn 2007; Slaney 1980) and it is is a lifelong process into work transition through choosing among plenty of employment opportunities.

Decisions regarding a future career are directly associated with a vocational identity. Career construction following the individual decision is a subjective matter based on 'a reflection of oneself' and the vocational identity of young person (Savickas, 2005, p. 54). The impact of career-related decisions has its long-lasting influence on personal life and self-fulfillment (Mann, Harmoni, Power, Beswick, & Ormond, 1988). While some make their choices rather easily, others face a career decision with serious vocational indecision, preventing them from successfully entering and completing the decision-making process.

A key turning point in adolescents' path of development is the vocation-related choice that they make while in high school. A young person undertaking the decision is influenced by many factors, such as the unique context of life, inborn and acquired talents or abilities, and educational success (Bandura, Barbaranelli, Caprara, & Pastorelli, 2001). Making a career decision is a complex process (Brown, 2002); hence adolescents facing the need to make a career choice encounter many common difficulties and go through more or less universal phases of the decision process.

As the crucial moment for youth is when they complete their secondary school graduation, they seek new opportunities in institutions of higher education or the workplace (Gati, & Ram 2000). Generally, youth find this difficult and seek professional counseling that will help them to identify themselves in the work environment (Walsh, & Osipow, 1988).

Vocational identity is a key issue for the ultimate choice of career. Vocational identity is specified by the possession of a clear and stable picture of one's goals, interests, and talents that finally lead to relatively untroubled decision-making and self-assurance in one's aptitude to make accurate decisions, despite some internal or external ambiguities (Gordon 1998; Holland, & Associates, 1980).

In some cases the identity-seeking process is disturbed by common difficulties such as placing the responsibility for one's own decision-making on someone else. Other individuals may tend to refrain, suspend or at least postpone the decision. All these quasi-solutions result in inadequate and frustrating situations that result in their life-long consequences.

An empirical study of Gati and his co-workers (Gati, Osipow, & Givon, 1995) presents a classification of difficulties related to decision-making about future career. What is career decision difficulty? It was defined as an insufficient awareness of the need to make a career decision or deficient capacity to make an appropriate and correct decision, which resulted in various mistakes such us incompatibility of individual's aspiration and the real resources of the adolescent.

Among many dysfunctions that may result in a wrong decision making process, Gati et al. (1995) classified inaccurate career decisions into some common and specific categories related to:

1. Lack of specific motivation and engagement in the decision-making process concerning professional career;

2. General indecisiveness related to any aspects;

3. Inappropriate beliefs and illogical expectations concerning the career decisions;

4. Lack or wrong information related to:
   - the steps involved in the process
   - self-knowledge (i.e., information about the career decision maker's preferences, values, abilities, etc.)
   - various alternatives concerning occupational knowledge (i.e., information about the alternatives of professional or educational paths or occupations)
   - procedural knowledge in reference to information about sources and skills to search necessary information

5. Problems concerning the use of information when there is excess of information or inconsistent and unreliable information about options of future study or work;

6. Internal conflicts and difficulties that compromise conflicting needs and aspirations;

7. External conflicts arising from the influence of parents, peers or other significant persons.

The presented taxonomy of the most frequent difficulties was confirmed by a study of Kleiman and Gati (2004).

As there are observable differences in the careers of men and women, there has been little attention paid to diversity related to gender differences in career decision taking. Studies of Gati et al. (1995) show that women and men still differ in their occupational choices; that is to say, women prefer a rather small repertoire and more traditional occupations and the occupations they choose tend to have lower salary levels than those of men. Research of Nevill and Schlecher (1988) indicates that women's choices have remained traditional and affected by sex roles and stereotypes in spite of recent social changes.

As mentioned in the previous section, career development might be seen as a decision-making process with a sequence of steps taken to work out a final career choice. Analogically to Ginzberg (1984) Three Stages Theory, an important observation is that career decision-making is a maturation process. The Prescreening, In-depth exploration, Choice model, called the "PIC model" by Gati and Asher (2001) consists of three main stages describing the career decision-making process, namely:

1. Prescreening stage where the individual searches and collects promising and viable career alternatives that deserve further, in-depth exploration. The prescreening stage also aims to eliminate impossible or disadvantageous options according to personal preferences and requirements (eg. high-school diploma, personality features or physical health, financial or time limitations). The significance of this stage lies in the fact that the final decision depends on the quality of the list of alternatives obtained at the end of the prescreening stage, and as such it is the critical phase for the whole decision making process;

2. In-depth exploration stage – a collection of comprehensive information about each of the promising alternatives and verification of their appropriateness and compatibility with the preferences. The young person tries to examine the ability to comply with prerequisites and required resources of the alternative explored. It consists of detailed comparisons of the most suitable alternatives and the selection of the most appropriate one. Another strategy of that stage is the ranking of all considered alternatives;

3. Choice stage – the individual is ready to indicate the most appropriate alternative to complete the career decision-making process.

The assistance of vocational counselors as well as more and more commonly used Computer-Assisted Career Guidance Systems (CACGS) may significantly increase life satisfaction by assisting youth in making good choices when entering the labor market (Gati, Saka, & Krausz, 2001). For example, it may be helpful especially at the initial phases of decision-making to provide alternatives and widen the repertoire of possible choice (Ballantine, 1986, Gati, Kleiman, Saka, & Zakai, 2003).

3. Theoretical background of the IPPJ questionnaire

Vocational assessment in career development and counseling is an essential challenge of career guidance. There would be no career counseling services without a reliable and valid diagnosis of one's own personal features and vocational preferences. One of the most ancient proverbs: *Nescete ipsum*[28] defines the path to successful and satisfactory life and work performance but also offers a clue to efficient career management. This quotation from Plato is closely associated with Super's perspective on the role of personal personality diagnosis, as he states that: "In choosing an occupation one is, in effect, choosing a means of implementing a self-concept" (Super, 1957, p. 196). But what is this *self* and personality while we relate them to work and occupation?

The Holland's theory aims to operationalize the concept of personality in the context of occupational preferences as the mode to grasp vocational preferences and serve in career counseling. According to Super, career choices are generally based on self-concepts projected onto career options.[29] This theory states that personality is the main creator of concepts that define the occupation which allows an individual to be the kind of person they seek to be.

The theory of Holland is derived from the most common concerns of vocational counselors and undoubtly each young person facing one of their most significant life-decisions. What is my occupational self concept? What kind of work do I need and seek? What are my real interests at work and career? All these questions have been channeled and expressed in Holland's attempt to operationalize and describe both the person and their work environment to successfully advise people in their career development.

3.1. The theory of John Holland

What is so important about Holland's theory (1997)? Holland's person and work environment typology is the most extensively analyzed and tested career theory. In addition, it presents a user-friendly and practically-oriented

---

[28] Know yourself.

[29] For young people, there is a great moment in the classic musical "The Sound of Music" when the hero tells the young Austrian soldier Rolf, "You'll never be one of them" (a Nazi), and he chooses to cling to his identity as being one of the Nazis.

approach to vocational counseling. This sum of research has discerned possible limitations, merits and challenges for future research on professional interests and counseling.

Holland's RIASEC[30] model has sometimes been maliciously called by its opponents the result of the globalization phenomenon of *McDonaldization* that also affected the career guidance. Presumably, this criticism may result from the shallow knowledge and limited expertise of the career-related theories and tools that have been created and improved for more than half century. It is rather more appropriate and efficient to assimilate all of what the discipline of vocational psychology has achieved and improve it, rather than simply reject the past to create 'new for new'.[31]

One of the most eminent contemporary researchers, Savickas, answered this concern by presenting a differentiated view of career intervention paradigms like vocational guidance, career education and career counseling and practices in counseling in indirect reference to the Holland's theory. With respect to Holland's theory, he asserted that 'Depending on a client's personal needs and social context, practitioners may apply career interventions that reflect different paradigms: vocational guidance to identify occupational fit, career education to foster vocational adaptation, or life design to construct a career story. Each paradigm for career intervention is valuable and effective for its intended purpose' (Savickas, 2012, p. 12).

What does Holland's theory state? The key concept of vocational personality (Holland 1959, 1997) implies that it is possible to identify 6 personality types, commonly abbreviated with the acronym RIASEC, which refer to the following personality types: Realistic, Investigative, Artistic, Social, Enterprising and Conventional.

Holland, as one of the first proponents of the person-environment fit in vocational psychology, proved its long-lasting impact, highlighting relevant aspects of the relation between personality and professional environment. According to Holland, 'The person making a vocational choice in a sense searches for situations which satisfy his hierarchy of preferred orientations' (Holland, 1959, p. 35). In other words, and on the basis of other related Holland's (1959) assumptions, the person somehow seeks to project their personality onto the best world of work. Individuals are attracted to a specific occupation that satisfies personal needs. Best person-work environment fit include career interest differences (Nauta, & Kahn, 2007), self-efficacy, and academic major-career congruence (Leong, 1991). Secondly, Holland stated that 'Persons with more information about occupational environments make more adequate choices than persons with less information' (Holland, 1959, pp. 40–41).

It is usually overemphasized that only Holland's theory permits the indication of a career-related personality. While vocational psychology offers many ways of assessing individuals at work, the major advantage and uniqueness of Holland's (1997) theory is that it enables us to describe environments. He has developed techniques for diagnosis and categorization of different work and occupational

---

[30] The Acronym for six personality and work environment types of Holland theory.

[31] It is worth considering that other theoretical concepts such as Prediger's model also provide empirical support for the RIASEC dimensions related as complementary to dimensions of *Data-Ideas* and *People-Things* (Prediger, & Vansickle, 1992).

environments. One of these tools is the *Position Classification Inventory* (G. D. Gottfredson & Holland, 1996), which describes work environments and classifies them according to RIASEC types as a complementary aspect to assess person-environment fit and set up valid and reliable predictors of vocational performance (L. S. Gottfredson, & Richards, 1999).

As the author presented his theory for the first time in 1959 in his article entitled, *A Theory of Vocational Choice* published in the *Journal of Vocational Psychology*, more than a half century later, it is obvious that Holland's typology has pervaded career counseling and become a turning point in professional guidance (Nauta, 2010). The fundamental assumptions summarized by Holland in 1997, have initiated a long and lasting study of professional career diagnosis and development.

The theory of vocational personality and work environment (Holland, 1959, 1985, 1997) has resulted in hundreds of research studies that have impacted vocational counseling practice psychometric tools[32] created on the basis of Holland's methodology. His theory is recognized as one of the most influential theoretical models that are commonly used in professional guidance.

A milestone of Holland's theory of vocational types and interests' development was the iconic hexagon model (Figure 5) which illustrated the possible typology of six kinds of occupations and their corresponding vocational personalities. (Holland, Whitney, Cole, & Richards, 1973). Holland assumes there are six vocational dominant personality types (identified by the types of interest) and six corresponding environments.

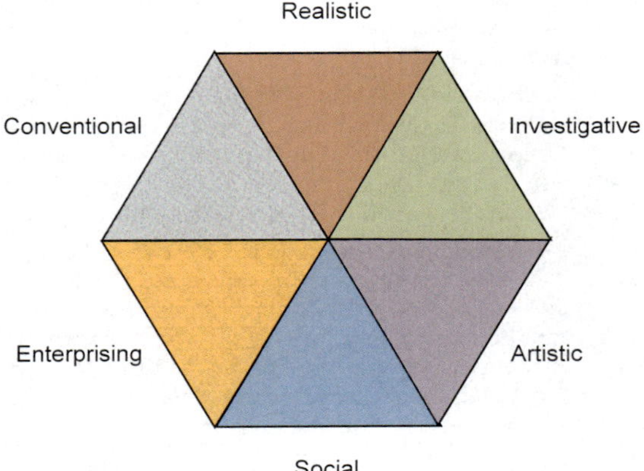

Figure 5. The hexagonal, RIASEC model of six vocational personality types (adapted from Holland, Whitney, Cole, & Richards, 1973)

The theoretical model confirmed by Holland's empirical study indicated six career type profiles with discriminative power to specify the level of coherence

---

[32] Such as the Self-Directed Search Test (SDS): Holland, J. L., Powell, A. & Fritzsche, B. 1994. *The Self-directed Search: Professional User's Guide*. Odessa, FL: Psychological Assessment Resources.

between an individual's personality and their most adequate work environment. Hence, for example, 'Realistic' types have their feet firmly fixed on the ground and are conforming; they prefer workplaces that require industrial or mechanical skill or are agricultural, whereas 'Artistic' types are creative, nonconforming, and emotional, prefer art and music as occupational choices (Holland, 1997). He also specified six environments easily mapped by six Holland's types with distinctive lifestyles, social skills, personal features and preferred work strategies and solutions while dealing with problems in each of the work environments.

The theory behind Holland's (1997) typology originated on personality typologies carried out by Adler, Fromm, Jung, Sheldon, Spranger, Murray, and Welsh. These authors led Holland to believe that it is possible to create an analogical typology for professional interests (as cited in Paszkowska-Rogacz, 2011). Professional personality types are estimated using interest items that express individual's preferences listed in the table below (Holland, 1997).

Table 5. Definitions of six RIASEC types

Realistic type (R) – represents people who like working with tools. They have usually manual skills in working with machinery and with tools, plants and animals. They are known as qualified, concrete, technical or mechanical. They like to work in professions such as measuring / surveying, agriculture, electricity and value practical solutions and things. Realistic type professionals generally avoid social activities related to healing, training and/or education
Investigative type (I)*– like to work with abstract concepts, and also have the talent to create theories and more abstract models. They try to understand the world by seeking the truth. They have mathematical and scientific interests and like to study science and solve math problems. They are described as rational, abstract, analytical and precise. They prefer scientific or intellectual jobs as biologist, physicist, chemist, medical technologist.
Artistic type (A) – prefer creative behavior like art, music, craft, drama or creative writing allowing free expression. They like to develop ideas and concepts characterized by originality and independence. They demonstrate different artistic abilities: literature, music or different visual arts. These people are considered to be creative, expressive, imaginative and aesthetic. They like to work in occupations such as: musician, painter, writer, interior decorator or designer, actor or journalist.
Social type (S) – This type of people want to perform activates to help other people such as to inform and teach others. They have developed interpersonal skills and are often more sensitive for other person's needs. They are known as cooperating, empathetic, patient, friendly and helpful. Social type professionals tend to look for occupations such as a teacher, a psychologist, a social worker, a judge. They like to perform activities like nursing, or giving first aid, teaching or providing information. Generally they avoid activities that require using machines, tools or technology. They are good teachers, psychologists, counselors or guides.
Enterprising type (E) – are people that enjoy working with people-oriented or material benefits. They have leadership and communication skills and like to lead and persuade people, and to sell either things or ideas. They are described as energetic, talkative, ambitious and usually they avoid activities that require careful observation and scientific, analytical thinking. As they value success in politics, leadership, or business, they are born to be leaders, salespersons, tour guide, or lawyers.
Conventional type (C) – people of this type are methodical and prefer to work with data, under orders and/or structuring them. They have the ability to work in an office and do accounting with numbers and different types of records and machines in a set and orderly way. They are described as organized and see themselves as orderly and good at following a set plan. Conventional type professionals like to work in occupations such as accountant, cashier, bank clerk, secretary.

* Holland previously named this type Intellectual (adapted from Holland, 1997)

As the person-environment congruence model implies some formal assumptions such as relative stability of career-related personality of the individual, most people can be categorized as one of six types: Realistic, Investigative, Artistic, Social, Enterprising, or Conventional. Correspondingly, there are six distinct model environments: Realistic, Investigative, Artistic, Social, Enterprising, or Conventional. According to Holland (1985), and persons with specified personality types seek out work environments congruent with their types, which let them perform and develop their skills and abilities, express their attitudes and values, and take on relevant roles (Holland, 1997). Finally, human behavior is determined by an interaction between personality and environment (Holland, 1997; Savickas, & Lent, 1994).

On the basis of the relation of certain vocational personality types or precise subtypes with appropriate and relevant environments, Holland's model enables satisfaction and performance in those work environments to be predicted. As such, all six types are operationalized and measured by interest items, assuming that they correlate with and express individual's personality traits (Holland, 1997). A vast corpus of research has supported the existence of Holland's hexagonal model and the applicative value of RIASEC types in various groups: high school and college students and workers representing various professional clusters.

The practical implications of the hexagonal theory are that it provides answers to 3 fundamental questions in career guidance: 1) What vocational personality traits and what work environment features impact the successful job fit that condition work involvement, personal satisfaction and high work performance? 2) What personal features condition stable and integral development of the individual in the specific work environment and what destabilize and frustrate personal needs? 3) How to support individuals in resolving their professional career dilemmas? These are basic challenges, among others, that vocational counselors encounter in the constantly changing nature of work and deep cultural shifts in social reality, education and the labor market.

3.2. Beyond the RIASEC code letters:
Diagnostic aspects of the profile

What do we learn from the hexagonal model by Holland (1997)? The hexagonal model had an enormous heuristic value for understanding the nature of professional preferences as it indicates six basic personality types and describes specific aspects of the work environments in which the individual functions. The theory of six vocational types is the only theoretical model that is a more or less successful attempt to link the concepts of vocational personality as well as work environment and as such support youth in the process of their successful career management.

One of Holland's theoretical model challenges is that there are no 'pure types' and *'many people resemble more than one, and in most cases all, of the types to a degree'* (Brown, 2002, p. 380). An individual's personality is rather a unique combination of many occupational types than a one discrete and isolated type. It implies the shift from a traits approach to a typology approach, where instead of a specific, discrete type we see a multidimensional profile based on the compound of simultaneously existing repertoire of more than one personality trait.

Since the individual may be described by more than one type, the result is shown in a pattern or sample of scores that is reflected in a combination of the letters of the RIASEC model. It may consist of a: 1. Four-letter code e.g. RECS (where the strongest features reflected in the model types are R-Realistic; E-Entrepreneurial; C-Conventional; S-Social); 2. Three-letter code (most commonly used) or two-letter, most practical summary code that describes the two highest RIASEC hexagonal model scores, e.g. AS, which means that the unique subtype of this person is A-Artistic and S-Social. As it was mentioned before, the RIASEC model also indicates the most adequate subtype of work environment for the individual; e.g. REC triad refers to the occupation that is describe by R-Realistic; E-Entrepreneurial and C-Conventional work characteristics.

The particular subtype is not the only information provided about the features imprinted in the profile representing the person and the work environment, and also its mutual fit. More diagnostic information may be provided from four other indicators derived from the Holland's (1997) theory, such as: (1) congruence, (2) consistence, (3) differentiation and (4) identity.

3.2.1. Congruence of professional interests

The congruence indicator refers to the degree of fit between the personality and work environment (Eggerth, 2008). Job satisfaction depends on the degree of correspondence of personality type and the occupational environment. To take conscious and adequate career decisions, it is important to have sufficient knowledge about oneself and the specific job position requirements. For instance, a highly congruent person would be an individual who had a three-letter code on the as Self-Directed Search Test (SDS) (Holland, Powell, & Fritzsche, 1994) of SER (S-Social; E-Entrepreneurial; R-Realistic) and is considering a career as a hospital administrator, which is also classified as SER.

As another example, a person with a personality type indicated by a higher score in the I-Investigative subscale is the most consistent with an investigative work environment, but the person with a type of R-Realistic has a least congruent match in the social environment.

Concerning this issue of person and job-characteristic fit Holland (1980) suggested 3 degrees of congruence between an individual's personality type and the type of environment: the highest level, for example, would be between A-Artistic personality type and A-Artistic like work environment; the second highest – between I-Investigative and R-Realistic types and/or the A-Artistic environment;

and the third, lowest level of congruence – eg. between the R-realistic personality type and the S-Social type (see Figure 6 and 7).

Analogically, there are more or less homogeneous work environments that impact on the level of *Congruence*. Homogeneous occupational environments may be described by one or two dominant types e.g. IA (high scores in I-Investigative and A-Artistic) and 4 weak types indicators SECR (S-Social, E-Entrepreneurial, C-Conventional, R-Realistic). In other cases one may deal with more complexes, diverse and less congruent job environments, which are represented by more than two dominant hexagonal types RIASEC scores.

Summing up, *Congruence* as a marker of fit between an individual's personality type and work environment type turns out to correlate with job satisfaction, career stability and work performance (Nauta, 2010).

3.2.2. Consistency of professional interests

Consistency is determined by the degree of inter-relation of types in the hexagonal pattern of personality or work environment (or college majors) namely, it refers to the internal coherence of an individual's subtype profile. There are 3 degrees of consistency: high, medium and low. A high degree of consistency occurs when an individual's pattern of personality traits types lies directly adjacent in the hexagonal model (see Figure 6). Hence we may see more or less similar types that describe the pattern of personality or work environment.

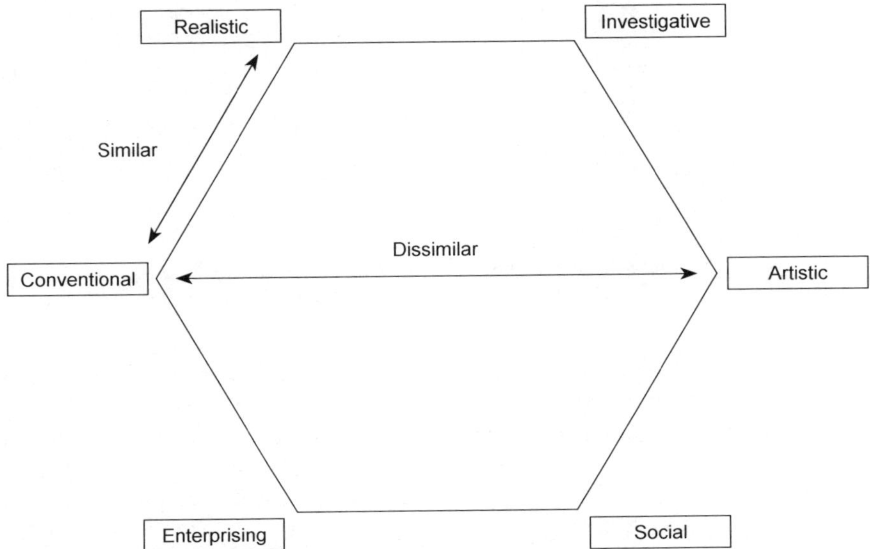

Figure 6. Similar and dissimilar types in the subtypes of hexagonal profiles
(adapted from Holland, 1997)

Consistency is estimated by determining the proximity of the strongest identified types that is first letters (the highest scores) of the three-letter code on the hexagon, e.g. SE: S-Social and E-Entrepreneurial personality are close in the RIASEC hexagonal, and constitute a consistent code for an individual (see Figure 7).

Consistency is a measure of the overlap and internal coherence of personality or work environment type as illustrated by the proximity of the hexagon presented in the types' scores. Adjacent types are more harmonious than types opposite each other in the hexagon, for example, Conventional and Artistic (CA). A person described by such a profile might experience constant distress or at least discomfort combining Conventional and Artistic interests, which are still rather rare cases in the repertoire of possible job options.

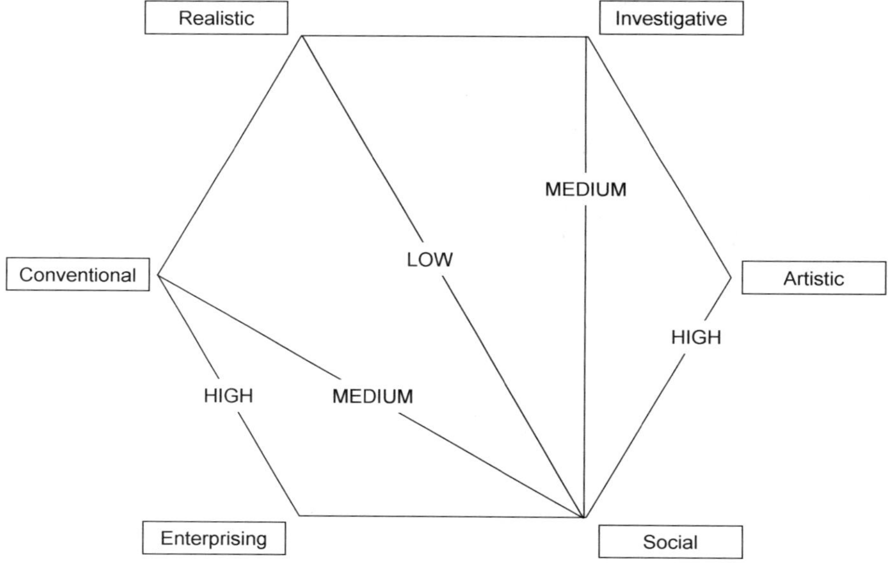

Figure 7. Three levels of consistency in the subtypes of hexagonal profiles
(adapted from Holland, 1997)

A person with a high level of consistency in his/her pattern of personality is characterized by a high degree of integration of the self, and his/her interests, system of values, personality traits and skills are harmonious and consistent. The behavior of such an individual is more predictable and allows for more appropriate occupational choices. A medium degree of consistency is characteristic for people whose personality constitute 'complementary types', such as Realistic and Artistic, which may enrich each other in some specific jobs characterized by more complex requirements. Some possible subtypes may also combine of a hexagonal pair of opposite personality types such as Conventional and Artistic. This situation may suggest that preferences of an individual may seem contradictory, and his/her professional choices are less predictable. Undoubtedly, people with incoherent personality type may have more difficulties in the professional orientation and decision process, but on the other hand, it is also an advantage for successful career development in the work environment that require a more complex, inconsistent and multifaceted set of personal interests and skills.

At present there is a growing number of particular jobs that require a combination of competence from distinct areas e.g. (RS) R-Realistic-S-Social type, e.g. dentist, physiotherapist, and for the (IE) I-Investigative-E-Entrepreneurial type e.g. social psychologist. Additionally, it can be expected that people with such a wide area of interests are able to think in a more inventive way and create new, interesting solutions. An inconsistent pattern may also mean that an individual may choose from a wide and varied range of professional options.

John Holland (1997) confirmed that very few researchers have taken an effort to verify the meaning of consistency in the development and stability of occupational patterns and the results obtained are not consistent or conclusive. Barak and Rabi (1981) and Wiley and Magoon (1982) conducted a study on the influence of the degree of coherence of the students' professional personality profile on their final exams results and received a positive association. Similarly, the study of O'Neil and Magoon (1977) showed the positive effect of consistency in career aspirations of students. Additionally, Aiken and Johnston (1973) provided empirical evidence that consistency allows to predict career decisions of work candidates with high probability.

Research of Holland, Sorensen, Clark, Nafziger and Blum (1973) as well as G. D. Gottfredson and Lipstein (1975) supported the idea of greater career stability of people with more consistent personality profiles. Simultaneously, the study of Erwin (1982) and Laton (1989) did not confirm the importance of stability for planning career development of students. In the last work of Holland (1997) he noted an interesting relationship – the role of consistency/inconsistency in career planning decreases with age. Additionally, the above mentioned studies (G. D. Gottfredson, & Lipstein 1975) confirm that the most predictive cases of personalities are characterized by coherent personality patterns and as such they appear to be the most stable professional career patterns.

Congruence described in the previous paragraph is partly related to the *Consistency* of hexagonal models, as the concept of consistency, can also be related and applied to types of the work environment. A consistent environment defines similar requirements, and offers similar benefits and work satisfaction for persons representing similar and consistent subtypes. For example, a CR work environment (C-Conventional and R-Realistic) is a consistent work context, as it requires analogous interests and abilities typical to these two types which condition high congruence of person and work environment.

To sum up, while the three first letters of the RIASEC model types are usually considered to determine *Consistency*, Holland (1997) recommends creating a professional personality portrayal of the individual based on the rank ordering of all six types.

3.2.3. Differentiation of vocational interests

The concept of *Differentiation* is related to the degree to which the person or the environments are clearly defined. It is a marker of the crystallization of preferences (Brawn, 2002). The *Differentiation* measure provides valuable information about the definition of adjacent types of the profile, namely it estimates the degree to which the individual or the work environment evidently resembles and adheres to some RIASEC types and not other ones.

Differentiation conditions the clarity with respect to professional choice (Nauta, 2010) and is the marker of a well developed vocational identity. A vocational differentiation problem may result in career indecision, role confusion, and negative mental health disorders such as depression, anxiety, and low self-esteem, hence successful differentiation is fundamental for achieving positive career outcomes (Strauser, Lustig, & Ciftci, 2008).

A clearly outlined personality profile is characterized by a high degree of similarity to one or two types, and a small degree of similarity to other types. In contrast, a poorly outlined personality profile shows a low degree of similarity to all types. *Differentiation* is a score calculated by subtracting from the highest ranking type result the lowest result among all six types or among the three scores of the three-letter code. The highest *Differentiation* represents a high level of association to types related to one similar preference category, whereas the lowest *Differentiation* would be illustrated by very similar scores in all hexagonal types (Brown, 2002). The objective and function of the differentiation indicator was plainly grasped by Holland: '*My purpose was to create a marker that would capture what counselors mean by a well-defined profile*' (Holland, 1997, p. 26).

In other words, *Differentiation* identifies the profile of the individual. When it is flat it shows little variation, while in case of a large difference between the highest and lowest it reflects a profile with a high degree of *Differentiation* (see Figure 8).

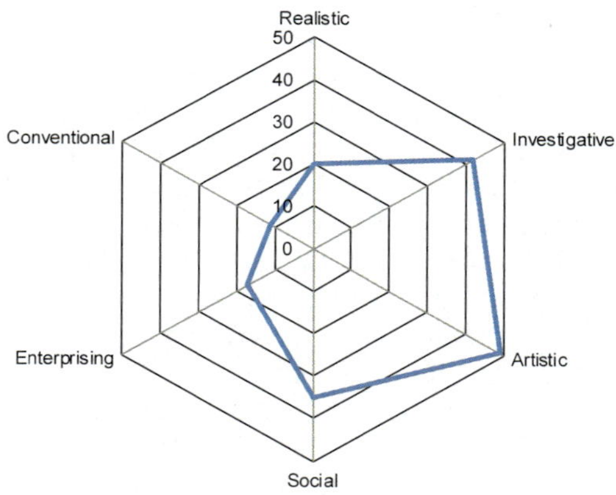

Figure 8. High differentiation RIASEC model types profile (adapted from Holland, 1997)

The higher the degree of differentiation and the more clearly a person is inclined toward the certain dominant type in their profile, the more clearly their preferences are defined. In a low differentiation profile, where the typical preferences are not crystallized yet, the individual has low scores in all 6 subscales on the 5-point scale, which is indicated in Figure 9.

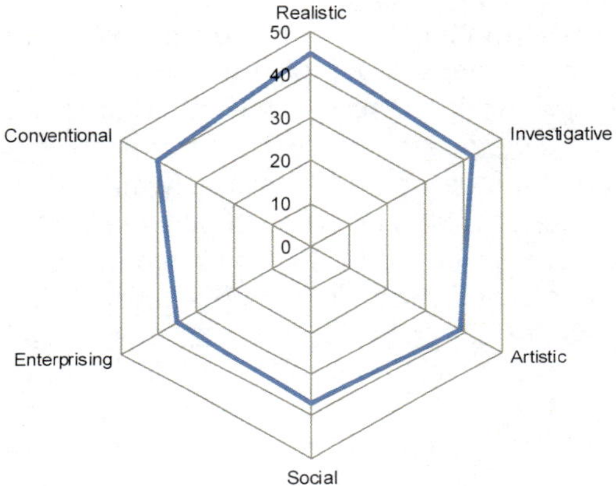

Figure 9. Low differentiation RIASEC model types profile (adapted from Holland, 1997)

Two indicators have been created by Holland and Iachan to assess the profile (Łącała, Noworol, Beauvale, 1998). The first, Holland's *Differentiation* indicator, is determined by subtracting the lowest result from the highest result of the RIASEC profile. The *Differentiation* indicator may be obtained from the difference of the highest and the lowest score among the six types or among the three scores making up the three-letter code. The highest *Differentiation* value would correspond to a high level of resemblance to one professional type, whereas the lowest would be a perfectly flat profile with similar scores in all six types.

Another way to estimate the *Differentiation* marker is Iachan's (1984) indicator, which is determined by the following mathematical formula (as cited in Łącała, Noworol, Beauvale, 1998):

$$L_1 = 1/2\,[X_1 - (X_2 + X_4)/2]$$

where:
X_1 = the highest score of the profile,
X_2 = the second highest scores of the profile,
X_4 = the fourth highest scores of the profile.

An additional valuable measure related to hexagonal scale is the indicator of the *Intensity of interest* which is a simple measure obtained by adding all six scores of the individual in the test of professional interests.

Studies carried out by Holland that aimed to analyze the degree of professional personality profiles differentiation as an independent variable showed a positive relation between the stability of occupational choice and the degree of differentiation (Łącała, Noworol & Beauvale, 1998). The longitudinal study by Taylor, Kelso, Longthorpe and Pattison (as cited in Holland, 1997) gave empirical evidence of that relation. In turn, Holland, G. D. Gottfredson and Nafziger (1975) found that this variable is positively correlated with the quality of decision-making and the consistency of occupational preferences.

The concept of differentiation also applies to work environments. Clearly outlined environments are generally represented by the 'one-type worker'. In heterogeneous and complex occupational environments, one can find employees representing a various constellation of all six personality types. Limited research takes into account both: the degree of consistency and differentiation profile, as the independent variables and results of existing studies are inconsistent or even contradictory. On the one hand, the study by Holland (1997) showed a positive cumulative effect of these two factors on the predictability of professional careers. On the other hand, studies by Villwock, Schnitzen, and Carbonary (1976) and Leung, Conoley, Scheel, and Sonnenberg (1992) did not confirm these relations. These conflicting results led researchers to find another independent variable that would hold more promise in prediction work congruence.

3.2.4. Identity and vocational interest

Identity has been most recently added as an indicator, and it assesses the extent of clarity of the *'picture of one's goals, interests and talents'* (Holland, 1997, p. 5), and/or it reflects to what extent a work setting has clear goals, tasks and rewards that remain stable over time (Nauta, 2010). *Identity* is somehow the function of *Differentiation* and especially *Consistency* indicators, as authors define it as the strength and distinctiveness of personalities and work environments (Brown, 2002). According to some research, *Consistency* and *Differentiation* have limited predictive power (Holland, 1997). In fact, Holland suggests replacing or at least complementing *Consistency* with the occupational *Identity* analysis. *Identity* is diagnosed by a special questionnaire on the *Vocational Identity (VI)* scale or another test: *My Vocational Situation* (Holland, G.D. Gottfredson, & Power, 1980). These questionnaires permit researchers and counselors to assess the crystallization of an individual's vocational identity and confront them with RIASEC codes of work environment based on job-analysis data. One of the most well-known publications commonly used by professional guides is the *Dictionary of Holland Occupational Code* (G.D. Gottfredson, & Holland 1996) or *The Educational Opportunities Finder* (Rosen, Holmberg, & Holland, 1997) based on the classification of 900 college majors including typical interests, skills, and abilities of the hexagonal model and academic majors related to each of six personality types.

On the basis of long-term empirical research, revisions and evolution in the development of the hexagon theory, Holland stated that *Congruence* is the most influential construct linking person and environment. *Differentiation* was in the second position of importance and *Consistency* was the least influential factor that conditioned the person-environment fit (Holland, Whitney, Cole & Richards, 1973).

The critical considerations of Mitchell and Krumboltz (1996) offer an analysis of the person-work environment theory. They state that in the context of rapid labor market and work environment changes as well as growing demands on individuals to change and adapt to their conditions, the usefulness of Holland's theory is limited. Other challenges for the RIASEC theory model are that general measures are insufficiently associated with gender, and additionally the fact that personality development might disturb the process of vocational choice on the basis of Holland's methodology (Osipow, & Fitzgerald, 1996).

As *Identity* is a complex and multidimensional aspect of professional career issues, it has been suggested those other relevant and useful variables such as: age, social class, and gender be controlled and analyzed. An important aspect of career identity is gender, as men generally tend to be interested in and choose Realistic types jobs, while women tend to score higher in Social (Paessler, 2015). Apart from that, occupational *Identity* seems to be conditioned by race and ethnicity, educational biography of individuals, previous work experience, peers beliefs and social trends, parent's professional or occupational profiles and possibly many other related factors that influence vocational identity and should be considered by counselors to appropriately and navigate youth's careers.

Finally, there is a broad field of study that examines the role of culture in professional identity construction, as a growing number of empirical studies challenge the universality of the hexagon model across cultures. The research of Fouad and Dancer (1992) and Rounds and Tracey (1996) provides evidence that culture and ethnicity influence the RIASEC profiles representing specific cultural groups.

To sum up, consistent and well-differentiated RIASEC subtypes tend to condition much more crystallized vocational identities of individuals. These persons are expected to make more accurate career choices with more efficiency to perform competent work with long-lasting satisfaction and engagement in appropriate social, organizational and educational behavior (Holland 1997).

3.3. Prediger's Model of work environment classification

One of the major aims and challenges of vocational guidance is to provide the vocational counseling client with a clear perspective on the complex occupational repertoire, with the goal of their adequate occupational positioning. Indisputably, Holland's model is the most widely used and influential occupational classification system applied in career guidance. The variety and the scale of the contemporary world of work require a well-thought-out and clear classification of possible professional paths that enables personally relevant job-related options to be identified, especially in the early stages of career planning.

Among a number of occupational classifications developed by professional guidance researchers, the World of Work Map Model by Prediger (Prediger, Swaney, & Mau, 1993) offers a valuable way to provide a comprehensive overview of the work world that may contribute to career exploration and planning. In spite of its strengths and weaknesses, Prediger's model helps to organize the complex world of work.

Prediger's World of Work Model corresponds and complements Holland's hexagonal model (Prediger, Swaney, & Mau, 1993; Prediger, & Vansickle, 1992). The World-of-Work Map's possible occupation areas are related to the U.S. job classification system (Bańka, 1995). A career area's location on the map is based on its primary work tasks. Prediger assumes that the selection of possible careers may be outlined in two bi-polar dimensions that imply the fundamental structure of six personality types identified by Holland (see Figure 10).

The position of each professional type is identified on the picture illustrating two basic dimensions, where the first is a domain ranging between people versus things, while the second dimension ranges in position between data and ideas.

The first dimension identifies preferences for occupations working with people (social type) versus those dealing with objects or machines (realistic type). Tasks oriented to people are related to teaching, communication, taking care of others. Working with objects implies working with tools and materials, e.g. metal, wood, repairing, and manufacturing or construction.

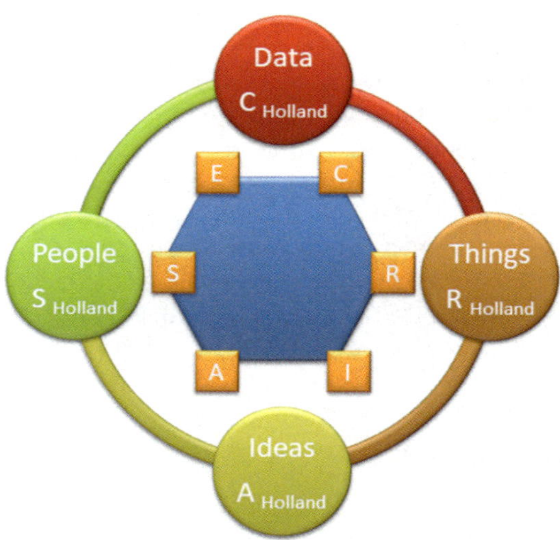

Figure 10. Integration of two job classifications by Holland and Prediger
(adapted from Holland, 1997 and Prediger, Swaney, & Mau, 1993)

The second dimension indicates preferred activities that imply either data or ideas and may be expressed in the interests for working with concrete data (Conventional and Enterprising type) rather than abstract concepts or more theoretical aspects (Investigative and Artistic types).

The bipolar nature of the two-dimensional space of professional interest means that scoring high on one end implies low scores on another end. People that tend to work with people would rather keep away from activities requiring work with objects, tools or machines and analogically, individuals interested in all activity types requiring abstract thinking and dealing with ideas would rather avoid conventional activities with concrete and defined data.

These two basic dimensions have been shown to underlie Holland's hexagonal model of vocational types in many empirical studies (Soulière, MacPhee, & Flynn, 1991) and the predictive validity of Prediger's bipolar work-task preference dimensions has been confirmed.

3.4. Typology of jobs according to Holland and Prediger

A theoretical model representing a possible job repertoire may systematize the reality of occupations, however counselors seek helpful concrete and operational advice in the face-to-face vocational encounter of the client and the professional counselor. As presented in Figure 11, Prediger's classification is coherent with and may be easily built into the hexagonal model, supporting Holland's intuitions related to fit of the personality (personal interests) and work environment (professional occupations).

The 'Work World Maps' model (Figure 12) positions 26 groups of model occupations representing sets of concrete professions. The classification illustrated below is based on the 'Dictionary of Occupations'[33] that categorizes all general professions according to the level of their similarity. Hence, all 'job families' imply their particular location on the circle/scheme according to the specificity of activities, interests and competences typical for individuals performing specific job.

Each section of the circle is represented by a certain group of jobs related to the hexagonal model of professional types:

"Business contacts" Group (Entrepreneurial Personality – E)
A. Marketing and Sales: vendor in shops, travel agents, salesmen, dealers, insurance agents, etc.
B. Management and Planning: heads of shops, hotels, farms, heads of offices, real estate agencies, managers in large companies, recreation services managers, city architects.

"Business operations" Group (Conventional Personality – C)
C. Accountancy and Communication: (e.g. office workers, postal office workers, receptionists, office and medical secretaries, orderlies)
D. Financial Transactions: (e.g. accountants, cashiers, usher, insurance agents);
E. Storage and Distribution: (e.g. officials sales, parcel carriers, logisticians, traffic controllers, truck drivers)
F. Operations of Computer and Data Processing: (e.g. specialists in offices, service photocopiers etc., typists, statisticians)

---

[33] US Department of Labor.

"Technical work" Group (Realistic Personality – R)

G. Vehicles: (e.g. vehicle drivers, mechanics, maintenance of forklifts, pilots of aircraft, naval officers)

H. Construction: (e.g. carpenters, electricians, painters, bricklayers, plasters, masons, building inspectors, metallurgists)

I. Natural Resources: (e.g. farmers, foresters, gardeners, retailers in pet shops)

J. Craft: (e.g. cooks, butchers, bakers, shoemakers, tuners musical instruments, tailors, jewelers)

K. Maintenance and Office Equipment: (e.g. TV servicemen, computers servicemen, telephones, air conditioning, office equipment)

L. Repair and Maintenance of Factory Equipment: (e.g. machine operators in factories, mines, etc., welders, printers, firefighters)

"Science" Group (Investigative Personality – I)

M. Engineering and other Applied Sciences: (e.g. engineers and technicians in various areas, laboratory technicians, computer programmers, nutrition technicians, experts)

N. Medicine: (e.g. orthodontists, EEG and EKG technicians, optometrists, orthodontists, radiologists, medical technicians, dentists, veterinarians, pharmacists)

O. Natural Sciences and Science (e.g. agricultural engineers, biologists, chemists, geographers, geologists, mathematicians, physicists)

P. Social Science: (e.g. market analyst, anthropologists, economists, psychologists, sociologists)

"Art" Group (Artistic personality – A)

Q. Applied Arts (Visual): (e.g. florist, interior designers, fashion designers, photographers, architects)

R. Arts: (e.g. entertainers, actors, musicians, singers, writers, art teachers)

S. Applied Arts (Verbal): (e.g. advertising agents, journalists, translators, lawyers, public relations staff)

Group "Working with people" (Social Personality – S)

T. Health: (e.g. nurses, physiotherapists, dieticians, speech therapists, doctors)

U. Education: (e.g. teachers, kindergarten teachers, sports coaches, university professors, teachers in special schools)

V. Social Services: (e.g. security personnel, police officers, health inspectors / food / safety, economists, social workers, therapists consultants).

W. Service Customers: (e.g. shopping packers, hotel messengers, office assistants, flight attendants, waiters, beauticians, hairdressers, maids)

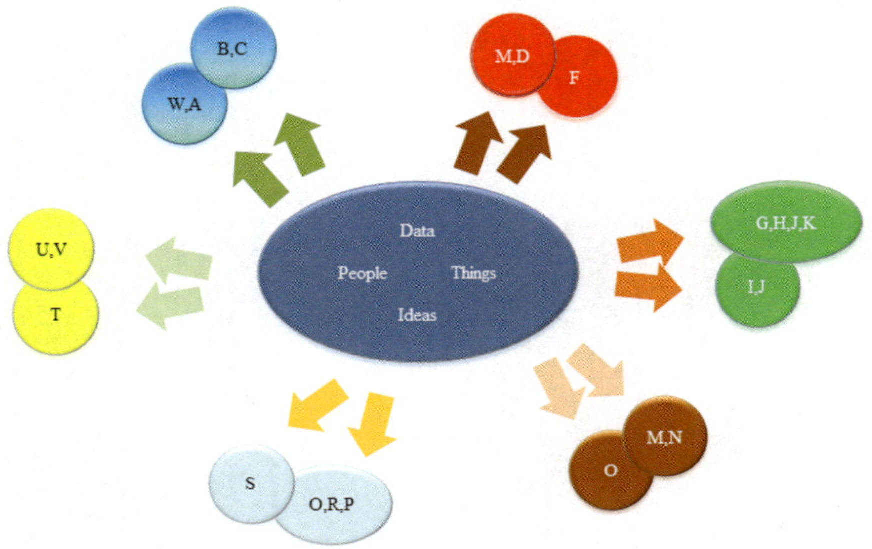

Figure 11. The World of Work Map (adapted from Prediger, Swaney and Mau, 1993)

"Business operations" (Conventional Personality C)
"Technical work" (Realistic Personality R)
"Science" (Investigative Personality I)
"Art": S,O,R,P: (Artistic personality A)
"Working with people" (Social Personality S)
"Business contacts" (Entrepreneurial Personality E)

The different colors in Figure 11 indicate 6 different RIASEC vocational types, while the letters (A,..., W) indicate the most typical occupations related to the Prediger's model of 'Data, Things, Ideas, People' model. As we see there is a thematic convergence of the two models that may better highlight the nature of distinct interests and occupations presented from the perspective of Holland's and Prediger's classification.

Beside the most commonly used Self-Directed Search by Holland (SDS; Holland, 1994) the Myers-Briggs Type Indicator (MBTI, Tieger, Barron-Tieger, 1999) is one of the most commonly used inventories in career counseling. These two models, the Self-Directed Search based on Holland's vocational theory and the MBTI, based on structural personality theory, have corresponding dimensions of personality traits (Chauvin, Müler, & Godfrey, 2010).

4. The design of the questionnaire

One of the most omnipresent determinants of research quality is its quantification; hence it was necessary to transpose the abstract concept of 'vocational preferences' into more operational and measurable units in a test form. In order to diagnose individuals' occupational interests, the research team undertook the complex process of operationalization of the concept of 'Vocational personality' (Holland, 1997). This process underlies the creation of the valid and reliable tool – *Inventario de las Preferencias Profesionales de los Jovenes en Ecuador* (IPPJ) – to support Ecuadorian youth in their successful school to work transition.

Questionnaire design was broken down into phases so that researchers would be able to estimate psychometric indicators and national norms to diagnose occupational interests of youth, and ultimately, to relate them to the most typical educational paths for secondary school graduates in Ecuador. This chapter will present the main phases of construction of the questionnaire for the diagnosis of career preferences of youth (16–18 years old).

The main activities related to the construction of the final version of the IPPJ tool were undertaken in accordance with the design standards of psychometric tools (Hornowska, 2007; Michell, 1999). The scale construction process was based on commonly used methodological strategies for creating psychometric tools designed for psychological measurement. The tool was created in cooperation with a team of 25 experts, psychologists presently employed in secondary schools in Ecuador as career counselors with experience in professional guidance.

According to Michell (1999) an important aspect of questionnaire construction is the diagnosis of specific traits in reference to the theoretical model that assumes specific definition of features, operationally defined by items. One of the preliminary phases of the test construction was the operationalization process of the concept of vocational preferences by six occupational types in the RIASEC model of Holland (1997) to indicate valid and reliable items related to the career interests of secondary school graduates.

The project design for the construction of the *Inventario de Preferencias Profesionales de Jovenes* was guided by the existing theories and models of vocational guidance described the prior chapter. The preliminary assumption of this undertaking was to create a socio-culturally valid, reliable and user-friendly tool that would be accessible to all vocational guidance related institutions to provide youth with a helpful guide to their vocational interests.

The questionnaire was created to serve all teachers, educators, and, in particular, a group of competent vocational counselors with a new instrument considered to be a 'career GPS' for Ecuadorian youth.

4.1. The construction of the pilot version

The personality type classifications created by Holland (1975) have gained the widest empirical confirmation and practical application and may be applied in the process of professional career prognosis and vocational counseling. The models served as a basis in the creation of the *Inventario de Prefencias Profesionales de Jovenes* (IPPJ) with most relevant items derived from the typology of professional interests suggested by Holland (1997) for the adequate diagnosis of personality type and prognosis of appropriate occupations in the future.

To minimize all possible errors in the assessment of vocational interests and determine valuable properties, including the confidence level of the tool results, the construction process established basic psychometric properties. This phase was designed to check whether the instrument actually measures what it sets out to measure (Criterion validity) and whether the tool's results can be interpreted consistently across different testing situations (Reliability).

Valid and reliable indicators of occupational interests that underlie the pilot version were in line with the hexagonal theory and definitions of 6 scales (see Table 5). The occupational interests' model (represented by the acronym RIASEC) is related to six personality types: 1. Realistic, 2. Investigative, 3. Artistic, 4. Social, 5. Enterprising, and 6. Conventional. Some more popular and commonly used descriptions of six types are by analogy: 1. Doers, 2. Thinkers, 3. Creators, 4. Helpers, 5. Persuaders, 6. Organizers (Johnson, 2013). The RIASEC types are used to describe not only professional personality types and work environments, but also college majors.

The process of generating possible items was based on typical indicators and expressions of professional types manifested at work, school, leisure and other relevant situations expressing specific occupation preferences of youth in Ecuador.[34] A team of 25 vocational guidance counselors were asked to create items according to the six definitions of career preference types and on the basis of items used in the pilot version of other tests based on Holland's model. After creating a first set of 180 items, the items were analyzed and assessed by professional counselors to decide whether they should be included in the pilot version. An important criterion in the process of item creation was the consideration of all significant socio-cultural aspects of the target group, namely young people aged 16–18 years.

---

[34] The RIASEC types are used to describe not only professional personality types and work environments, but also college majors (Harrington, Feller, & O'Shea, 1993).

After the first process of generating 180 items, 150 items were preliminarily selected to undergo an in-depth qualitative and quantitative questionnaire analysis and assessment. The group of 25 psychologists analyzed the quality and the level of adequacy of each item in the context of all six vocational personality types.

The qualitative analysis of items considered the following aspects:

1. Discriminative power of items related to all six professional preferences;
2. Analysis of the vocabulary (avoiding unclear concepts);
3. Analysis of grammatical correctness of items;
4. Formal simplicity of items;
5. The introspection skills of youth 16–18 years old;
6. Avoiding negative forms of items or double negation cases;
7. Socio-cultural aspects of the language and life style of youth;
8. Educational context of youth in Ecuador;
9. The reality of the labor market in Ecuador and existing professions;
10. Avoiding redundant items and looking for different forms of the operationalization of each of 6 professional types;
11. Using two gender forms of items, etc.

A parallel quantitative analysis performed by 25 vocational counselors after the qualitative study of items allowed for the assessment of the level of relevance of each item for each of six RIASEC subscales on a 5-point scale (from totally irrelevant [1] to totally relevant [5]). The psychometric analysis was based on two statistical indicators: the Mean (M) and the Standard Deviation (SD) of the competent judges' assessment of each item. The minimum Mean value applied to accept the item was not less than 3.9 (M> 3.9) on the 5-point scale and the Standard Deviation below 1.3 (SD<1.3).

After the analysis of 180 items, the set of 120 best items was finally defined, with 20 items for each of six professional types. In the final items set for the pilot version, 126 items were used. Six items were repeated to indicate the reliability based on the assessment of the same items and evaluate internal reliability of the test by checking the correlation of the same 6 items. Hence the final number of items in the pilot version was 126 items, however only 120 were included in the final calculations.

An important element of the construction of the pilot version of the tool and its qualitative assessment was the analysis of different versions and determination of the final version of the instructions, which were analyzed and discussed in a collegial way by a team of competent judges. A pilot version of the questionnaire was based on a 5 point Likert scale measurement. Respondents were asked to assess their opinion by selecting 1 of 5 possible answers: 1 – strongly disagree, 2 – disagree, 3 – hard to say, 4 – agree, 5 – totally agree.

4.1.1. The pilot study

The pilot study was planned as a preliminary test conducted on the relevant group of students to evaluate the tool's feasibility and to receive feed-back about the form of the questionnaire. It also aimed to observe the internal structure concerning Holland's theoretical model (1997) and to assess if is ready and appropriate for the performance of a full-scale research project. In other words, the main objectives of the pilot study were to:

1. Test the validity of the questionnaire related to the hexagonal model of Holland's typology of professional preferences;

2. Identify the final items set of each of 6 professional types of RIASEC model according to statistical indicators;

3. Exclude items that were incomprehensible to subjects;

4. Assess the general attitude of respondents in regard to the questionnaire with two questions, asked after completion of the questionnaire: (a) What do you like about this questionnaire? and (b) What don't you like about this questionnaire?

The group of 8 investigators conducting the study was prepared during two instruction workshops to standardize the pilot study procedure in strict cooperation with the coordinating team of SNNA (*Sistema Nacional de Nivelacion and Admision*) and Mariusz Wołońciej (Prometeo). The pilot study was conducted on a representative group of 1317[35] secondary school students from eight randomly selected schools[36] in Pichincha Province in Ecuador.

The study results were conducted and collected over a period of three days, from 1–3 of October, 2013 by a team of 8 vocational counselors working in selected secondary schools in the Province of Pichincha:

1. Unidad Educativa La Concordia;
2. Unidad Educativa José María Velaz;
3. Colegio Juan Pio Montúfar;
4. Colegio Sagrados Corazones de Rumipamba;
5. Colegio Militar Eloy Alfaro;
6. Unidad Educativa Nanegalito;
7. Spellman;
8. Unidad Educativa Municipal San Francisco de Quito.

A random representation of secondary schools was designed in regard to the following Ecuadorian school types: 1. Fiscal (3 schools); 2. Particular (2 schools); 3. Fiscomisional (2 schools); 4. Municipal (1 school). The number of randomly selected students from each school is presented in table 6.

The students of the 8 Pichincha schools incorporated in the randomly selected province of the pilot study were residents of 21 of all 24 provinces of Ecuador (see Tables 7 and 8). The number of students, considering their place of residence, was not well represented by all provinces, however, as the highest number of students had a place of residence in Pichincha (892 students; 67,7%), Santo Domingo de los Tsáchilas (165; 12,5%) and a very low number of respondents were from

---

[35] The total number of students enrolled in the sample was 1466, but because of the missing data 1317 were finally included in the statistical analysis.

[36] The random selection was conducted by *Sistema Nacional de Nivelación y Admision* administration to ensure that all schools and students be provided equal opportunity to be included in the pilot study program considering the types of school, the region (urban and rural) and type (public, private).

other provinces. The province of residence was not considered a very relevant variable in the pilot study, however. This sample allowed for the assessment of the pilot version on the group of youth attending the last class of the secondary school (age 16–19 years).

Table 6. The number of students included in the pilot study and representing each of secondary schools by school types

Institution	School code	Status	Province	Nr. of students
Unidad Educativa La Concordia	1	Fiscal	Pichincha	429
Unidad Educativa José María Velaz	2	Fiscomisional	Pichincha	36
Colegio Juan Pio Montúfar	3	Fiscal	Pichincha	286
Colegio Sagrados Corazones de Rumipamba	4	Particular	Pichincha	107
Colegio Militar Eloy Alfaro	5	Fiscomisional	Pichincha	212
Unidad Educativa Nanegalito	6	Fiscal	Pichincha	43
Spellman	7	Particular	Pichincha	132
Unidad Educativa Municipal San Francisco de Quito	8	Municipal	Pichincha	72
Total				1317

Table 7. Structure of the sample of students in regard to the place of residence in a study of the pilot version of the IPPJ questionnaire

Province	No	%
1. Azuay	7	.5
2. Bolívar	5	.4
3. Cañar	1	.1
4. Carchi	6	.5
5. Chimborazo	10	.8
6. Cotopaxi	17	1.3
7. El Oro	10	.8
8. Esmeraldas	72	5.5
9. Galápagos	2	.2
10. Guayas	13	1.0
11. Imbabura	11	.8
12. Loja	17	1.3
13. Los Ríos	10	.8

Table 7. cont.

Province	No	%
14. Manabí	25	1.9
15. Orellana	1	.1
16. Pastaza	2	.2
17. Pichincha	892	67.7
18. Santo Domingo de los Tsáchilas	165	12.5
19. Sucumbíos	5	.4
20. Tungurahua	11	.8
21. Zamora Chinchipe	1	.1
Total	1317	100

Considering the variable to school type: public (*Publica*), private (*Particular*) and semi-private (*Fiscomisional*), the majority of students were from the public schools (N = 758; 58%), with semiprivate schools (N = 248; 18.8%) and private schools (N = 311; 23.61%) at a lower representation level in the sample.

Table 8. Structure of the sample of students in regard to the type of educational support in 2011–2012

Type of education	Number of students	Number of students in special education	Total	%
Semiprivate	204.332	68.127	272.459	6.2
Private	917.972	94.747	1.012.719	22.9
Public	3.013.634	120.101	3.133.735	70.9
Total	4.135.938	282.975	4.418.913	100.0

Source: AMIE-MinEduc/Proyección de población-INEC 2012.

Educational Institutions (IE) included in the sample are classified according to the main source of financial support. By this criterion they were defined as public (*fiscal*), or private (*privado*) or public with private financial help (*fiscomisional*) according to the regulations of the Ecuadorian Constitution (2008): Article 345 and LOEI: Art. 53, 54, 55 and 56. The number of students involved in the pilot study sample is close to the general representation of Ecuadorian schools according to the type of financing (Table 8).

The random selection was conducted by the office of *Sistema Nacional de Nivelación y Admisión* (SNNA SENESCYT) to ensure that all school types were provided equal opportunity to be included in the pilot study program considering the profile of schools: general, technical, artistic, international; the region: urban and rural, and funding type: public, private, semi-private and one municipal school (see Table 8). The sample consisted of 172 students who attended technical schools and 1141 attended general education schools. Considering the area of residence: 979 students lived in cities and 325 in rural areas.

4.1.2. The validity study

Validity is one of the key criteria of the test's quality. While the name of the tool *Inventory of the Occupational Preferences of Youth* [*Inventario de Preferencias Profesionales de los Jovenes*] assumes that it measures occupational preferences (face validity), only empirical examination of the factor structure (latent variables) of the questionnaire may allow the test to be regarded as a valuable and useful tool in assessing the interests of youth.

In order to check the area of test application of the *Inventario de Preferencias Profesionales de los Jovenes*, i.e., what it measures and how well it does, factor validity and content validity were assessed, and, in the next stage, the questionnaire's reliability was also estimated. These criteria determine the correctness of the conclusions derived from the results of the IPPJ questionnaire and its applicability in vocational guidance of high school graduates and other respondents in Ecuador.

Unfortunately, in Ecuador no relevant and psychometrically justified tools were available for parallel testing of the same construct of professional types according to the Holland's model. As the purpose of the validation was to verify the accuracy of the internal structure of the questionnaire, exploratory Factor Analysis (FA) was conducted. FA is commonly used in the development of an instrument as it is useful for exploring patterns in a set of correlation coefficients. This analysis uncovers the underlying structure of latent constructs underlying the factors structure and identifies the best items to be included in the test. The final version of the test consists of items characterized by sufficiently high reliability and is based on internal consistency of each scale and results stability. To test the hypothesis that the model fits the data, confirmatory factor analyses was also carried out.

At this stage of the development of the scale, preliminary intergroup differences (e.g. gender, profile of the school) were also assessed as an additional indicator of the tool. This kind of validity indicators determine whether the test result may be regarded as a basis for making predictions, assuming that people with different test results will tend to behave in a different way (Brzeziński, 2006; Field, 2005). Concurrent validity obtained in this way allows for the estimation of the predictive validity to be defined on the basis of the test results in the context of other test results (other occupational type scores).

Content validity analysis allowed to assess the level of relevance and representation of each item in relation to each of six professional types to be identified, as well as a typical set of occupational behaviors for each of the types (Ferguson, & Takane, 1999; Field, 2005).

It is worth considering and resolving methodological doubts – whether the proportion of the sample size to the number of claims is correct. In the relevant literature, one can meet various recommendations. Most strict researchers suggest conducting a study on a sample with 10 times more respondents than variables (Hornowska, 2007; Nunally, 1978). Other researchers have less strict requirements; however, e.g., Kass and Tiensley (1979) argue that 5 to 10 respondents for each variable is a sufficient number, adding that the minimum sample number should be 300 respondents. Similarly, Comrey and Lee (1992) consider the number of 300 respondents as a sufficient sample size, but not less than 100. Cattell (1978) argues that the proportion of the sample size to the number of variables should be 3 to 6 respondents for each variable, and Ho (2006) mentions the rule according to which the factor analysis should meet two criteria: the sample should consist of at least 100 people, and each item should be represented by at least 5 respondents. Following these less restrictive assumptions, it should be considered that in the context of the selection criteria mentioned above, the sample of 1317 subjects fulfills all necessary initial criteria for conducting a factor analysis with 6 factors defined.

As described in the previous chapter, 1466 high school students participated in the pilot study. After the exclusion of 149 incorrectly filled sheets, the final sample consisted of 1317 students between 15 and 24 years (M = 16.91; SD = 0.88). All schools included in the study sample were randomly selected from the Province of Pichincha. Table 9 presents the number of girls and boys included in the test validity study.

Table 9. Structure of the sample tested in the
a pilot version of the IPPJ questionnaire, by gender

Gender	N	%
Girls	529	40.1
Boys	788	59.9
Total:	1317	100.0

Factor Analysis of the 120-items version permitted the assessment of items in regard to the content of the indicated factors (latent variables). The factor analysis fulfilled necessary statistical requirements and conditions. To ensure satisfactory methodological standards, all necessary requirements were included in the analysis. Foremost, the sample significantly exceeded the required minimum number of respondents (300) (see Tabachnick, & Fidel, 2007).

Secondly, the quality of analysis was tested with regard to measures of Factor Analysis appropriateness by *Kaiser-Meyer-Olkin Measure (KMO) of Sampling Adequacy*. The *KMO* test verifies the ability to efficiently factorize the originally assumed variables. As correlation between two variables can be also influenced by the others, partial correlations were estimated in order to measure the relation between two variables, removing the effect of the remaining variables. The KMO indicator was .94, by far sufficient, permitting the application of *Factor Analysis* and avoiding the necessity of examining the *Anti-Image Correlation Matrix* (Comrey, & Lee, 1992).

The value of the KMO statistic can range from 0–1; a value close to 1 indicates that the internal structure of variables obtained in Factor Analysis is clear and reliable. Kaiser (1974) recommends relying on a KMO value greater than .50; however Hutcheson and Sofroniou (1999) consider values above .90 to be outstanding.

Thirdly, the *Bartlett Sphericity Test* permitted calculation of the correlations between the variables and a comparison of the observed correlation matrix to the identity matrix to check the redundancy between the variables. The *Bartlett Sphericity Test* demonstrated that the identity matrix on the main diagonal had a value of 1, while the rest of the matrix was filled with zeros. This means that no correlation between variables was present (see Field, 2005), $\chi2 = 66333.130$, $p < .0001$.

Factor Analysis is a statistical method based on a correlation matrix of all items and serves to indicate latent variables called factors. *Exploratory Factor Analysis* was conducted using *Principal Component Analysis* (*PCA*) with normalized, *Standard Promax Rotation*. A rotation test served to make it easier to identify the internal structure on the basis of the loadings pattern, where the strongest items create distinct factors.

Rotation was chosen due to the possible correlation of factors, and assumptions made to adapt it for large data sets. The analysis of Crabtree (Weinrach, 1984) justifies the use of the correlation technique in this situation. The study of Crabtree done in 1971 gave evidence for high correlations (.40 to .71) between adjacent vocational personality types in Holland's hexagonal model.

The Factor Analysis of the 120 items included in the pilot version of the test indicated 21 principal components with the *eigenvalue* (*factor loads*) above 1, explaining 60.83% percent of the total variance. As the existence of six factors had been assumed – the hypothetical hexagonal model was confirmed empirically.

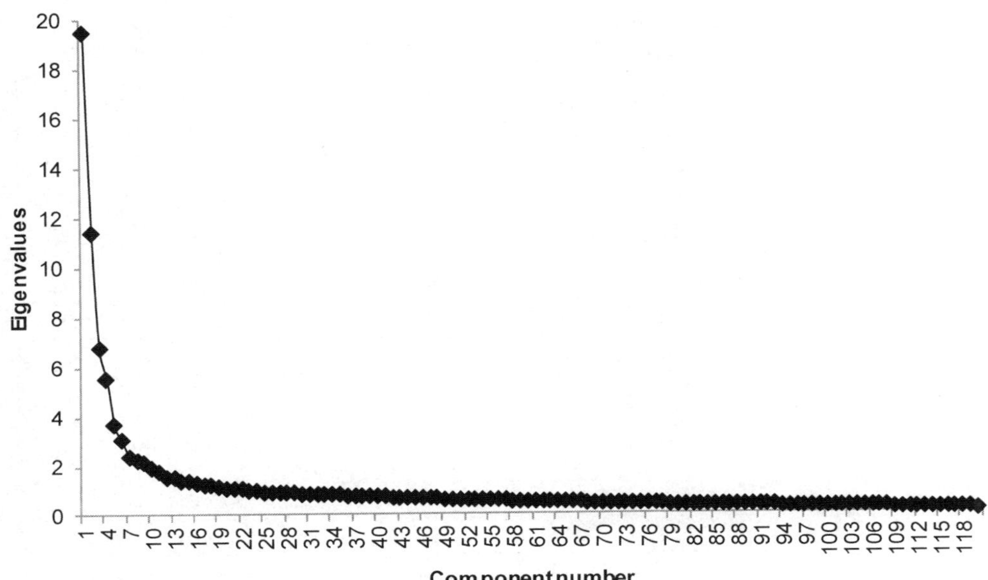

Figure 12. Scree plot of *Factor Analysis* for the 120-item version (pilot version)

The graph scree (Figure 12) clearly indicated between 6 or 7 major factors, listed in table 10. Together, these 6 factors explained 41.96%, of the total variance while the first factor explained 16.45% (eigenvalue was 19.74), the second: 9.56% (eigenvalue was 11.48), for the third: 5.60% (eigenvalue was 6.68), for the fourth: 4.75% (eigenvalue was 5.70), the fifth: 3.08% (eigenvalue was 3.69) and the sixth: 2.86% (eigenvalue was 3.06). Pilot study results confirmed the theoretical assumption of the hexagonal model of professional preferences according to the model of Holland (1997).

Content analysis allowed each factor to be assigned to its respective scale: 1 – Realistic (R), 2 – Enterprising (E), 3 – Social (S), 4 – Artistic (A), 5 – Innovation (I) and 6 – Conventional (C).

Table 10. Factor loadings for distinct items after rotation in the 120-item pilot version[37]

Items	Factors					
	1 (R)	2 (S)	3 (E)	4 (I)	5 (A)	6 (C)
1	2	3	4	5	6	7
R_93	.826	−.147	−.019	.142	.082	−.120
R_63	.825	−.116	−.007	.134	.037	−.114
R_23	.779	.141	−.126	−.021	−.044	.021
R_111	.779	−.103	−.028	.111	.053	.013
I_73	.742	−.077	.002	.082	.173	−.135
R_35	.730	−.020	−.020	.047	−.020	−.103
R_99	.717	−.104	−.051	.131	.008	.101
R_105	.706	.020	−.077	.063	.010	−.200
I_61	.696	−.152	.130	.172	.023	−.058
R_17	.665	−.025	−.086	.089	.135	−.035
C_46	.603	.295	−.067	−.054	−.044	.031
C_86	.569	.154	.118	−.016	−.181	.139
R_47	.563	.004	.066	−.070	.174	.045
R_75	.562	.013	−.197	−.044	.353	.138
C_92	.549	.257	−.007	−.192	−.130	.164
R_81	.543	−.231	.109	.083	.053	.027
R_41	.461	.133	−.124	.134	.239	−.172
I_9	.460	−.176	.017	.156	.105	.176
E_64	.457	.132	.290	−.222	−.081	.099
I_3	.424	−.337	.170	.005	−.083	.192
C_80	.424	.419	.016	−.199	−.162	.077

[37] As 6 repeated items of the total 126 set of items in the pilot version were excluded.

1	2	3	4	5	6	7
R_57	**.408**	−.068	.003	.137	.091	.002
E_70	**.347**	.015	.300	−.125	−.117	.132
C_16	**.316**	.224	.055	−.082	−.139	.278
R_29	**.310**	−.054	.057	.101	.086	.260
I_55	**.236**	−.056	.071	.200	.171	.152
E_2	**.217**	−.041	.206	−.076	.031	.187
S_59	−.037	**.724**	−.122	.123	−.055	.033
S_89	−.073	**.714**	−.112	.313	−.068	.073
S_53	.027	**.709**	.070	.109	−.051	.084
S_101	.260	**.693**	.021	−.010	−.039	−.118
S_18	−.006	**.652**	.092	.044	−.010	.010
S_65	−.066	**.647**	.346	.038	−.084	−.125
S_6	−.064	**.601**	−.130	.259	−.083	.069
S_48	−.044	**.597**	.190	.060	−.010	.081
S_119	−.096	**.590**	.424	.137	−.145	−.179
S_107	−.122	**.583**	.241	.216	−.023	−.076
A_54	−.057	**.576**	−.177	−.163	.161	.077
S_42	−.164	**.546**	.167	.097	.048	.035
A_60	.000	**.503**	−.138	−.165	.296	.031
R_52	.115	**.500**	−.196	.330	.093	−.045
A_108	.038	**.499**	.005	−.197	.311	−.049
R_69	−.140	**.497**	−.160	.360	.172	.179
S_24	−.166	**.466**	.044	.290	.103	.007
S_36	−.017	**.461**	−.051	.061	−.159	.332
A_78	−.009	**.455**	−.020	−.194	.307	−.044
A_66	−.004	**.452**	.050	−.176	.364	−.055
S_71	−.087	**.361**	.314	.307	.047	−.108
R_11	−.065	**.339**	−.182	.338	.166	.043
A_43	.003	**.318**	.076	−.103	.161	.136
E_88	−.016	**.317**	.286	−.104	.164	.069
C_62	.219	**.273**	−.226	−.092	−.108	.206
E_32	−.107	−.159	**.699**	−.013	.060	.073
E_112	.121	.145	**.650**	−.051	−.136	−.134
E_83	−.066	−.166	**.625**	−.004	.134	.113
E_100	.079	.135	**.603**	−.084	−.035	−.147
E_44	−.097	.058	**.595**	.017	.038	.095

Table 10. cont.

1	2	3	4	5	6	7
E_20	−.009	−.020	**.688**	−.042	.103	−.125
E_120	.154	−.041	**.678**	−.033	−.102	−.115
E_118	−.013	.201	**.515**	−.072	−.126	.047
E_14	−.017	−.051	**.509**	.067	.031	.058
I_15	.029	−.130	**.506**	.171	.034	−.033
I_39	−.091	−.150	**.504**	.141	.086	.133
S_12	−.115	.153	**.501**	−.002	−.009	−.062
E_106	.009	.248	**.482**	−.169	.105	−.127
E_58	.320	−.017	**.469**	−.040	.029	.038
I_27	−.035	−.173	**.469**	−.017	.127	.178
E_76	.098	.264	**.465**	−.021	.001	−.020
E_26	.000	.105	**.464**	−.072	.156	.097
S_77	−.170	.206	**.461**	−.005	−.003	.085
E_94	.021	−.071	**.442**	.055	−.038	.309
S_113	−.117	.382	**.405**	.064	−.018	−.029
I_33	−.128	−.185	**.397**	.213	.126	.199
I_21	.062	.004	**.383**	.050	.140	.094
A_37	−.006	.014	**.377**	.012	.341	−.076
S_95	−.002	.341	**.377**	.098	.107	−.115
S_83	−.104	.215	**.331**	−.008	.094	.260
E_38	.143	.124	**.261**	.052	−.002	.076
S_30	.006	.172	**.241**	.111	−.041	.234
I_97	.045	.175	−.013	**.798**	−.054	−.081
I_109	−.050	.300	.064	**.758**	−.117	−.131
I_50	.153	.184	−.062	**.738**	−.049	−.073
I_115	.282	.012	.034	**.725**	−.074	−.051
I_67	.215	−.121	.085	**.719**	.029	−.010
I_103	−.020	.389	−.058	**.707**	−.052	−.044
A_102	.059	.212	−.060	−.077	**.732**	−.048
A_31	−.070	−.001	.190	.015	**.714**	−.018
A_90	.201	−.001	−.008	.026	**.694**	−.123
A_72	.158	−.020	−.008	.050	**.683**	−.153
A_25	−.054	.005	.037	.099	**.585**	.136
A_114	.005	.298	.109	−.188	**.579**	−.127

1	2	3	4	5	6	7
I_79	.100	−.005	.048	**.693**	.096	−.019
I_85	.150	−.105	.045	**.662**	.073	.064
I_45	.151	.015	.013	**.657**	−.030	.121
R_87	−.094	.262	−.184	**.382**	.273	.213
A_13	.011	−.168	.094	.063	**.578**	.113
A_19	.254	.023	.096	.116	**.553**	−.209
A_49	.200	.064	−.001	−.062	**.508**	.103
A_96	.178	.298	−.121	−.038	**.451**	.063
A_1	−.034	.185	.237	−.092	**.384**	−.017
R_117	.156	.144	−.119	.025	**.383**	.254
I_91	−.143	−.093	.098	.036	**.313**	−.031
A_7	.186	.191	.171	−.222	**.299**	−.019
A_84	−.069	.122	.196	−.028	**.268**	.252
C_68	−.086	.012	−.149	−.079	.080	**.790**
C_116	−.069	.081	−.106	−.110	.077	**.782**
C-4	−.275	.010	−.081	−.052	.111	**.717**
C_10	−.078	−.075	.094	.010	−.010	**.646**
C_56	−.070	−.073	.065	.083	−.011	**.602**
C_104	.014	.058	.104	−.024	−.057	**.592**
C_51	.217	.218	−.162	−.056	−.080	**.495**
C_98	.084	.065	.098	.002	−.067	**.485**
C_74	.194	.041	.098	−.096	−.048	**.475**
C_110	.097	−.162	.226	.086	−.062	**.462**
C_28	.159	.152	.031	−.038	−.236	**.425**
C_34	.241	−.002	.051	.091	−.161	**.391**
C_40	.190	−.001	.104	.085	−.091	**.375**
C_22	.094	.002	.192	−.014	−.016	**.366**
R_5	−.215	.078	.063	.227	.187	**.267**
E_8	−.105	−.086	.148	.063	.151	**.203**

Designation of load factors: R – Realistic, I – Innovative, A – Artistic, S – Social, E – Enterprising, C – Conventional; the bold font indicates factors

After factors were extracted the degree of distinct item load on these factors was calculated. Each of the 6 factors consists of 10 items (all items with codes are included in Appendix 4) and they are indicated in bold font in table 10. On the basis of collected observations regarding the test with the 120 item version, some practical recommendations were made to decrease the total number of items as respondents complained it was too long and repetitive, although from a statistical point of view most of the total set of 120 had satisfactory markers (Table 10).

Correlation analysis between 6 factors showed that some factors were positively correlated, though most correlation values were relatively low (Table 11), which confirms the independence of distinct dimensions. There are also factors with higher correlation values, and this may be theoretically explained (Holland, 1997).

Table 11. Matrix of correlation (r Pearson) between factors in the 120-item pilot version

Factors	Realistic	Social	Enterprising	Investigative	Artistic	Conventional
Realistic	1.000	−.016	.188	.162	.080	**.266**
Social		1.000	.377	−.010	**.405**	.192
Enterprising			1.000	.117	.208	**.437**
Investigative				1.000	.084	.230
Artistic					1.000	.032
Conventional						1.000

Designation of load factors: R – Realistic, I – Innovative, A – Artistic, S – Social, E – Enterprising, C – Conventional

The orthogonal rotation assumes that all factors are rather independent, or unrelated. Beside the assumption of the factors' independence there are some theoretical reasons to suppose that the factors might be related as we have in case of the relation between Conventional and Enterprising (.437) or correlation between Artistic and Social professional personality types (.405) or between Realistic and Conventional (.266). All indicated and significant correlations may be related to the nature of occupational types and interests that is rather a complex flux than a well-organized structure of distinct and independent dimensions. Nowhere, neither in theory nor in the vocational guidance experience, has it been found that occupational interests are absolutely independent of each other, although Holland's model assumes the discriminative power of the RIASEC model. This comes from the intrinsic complexity of professional performance that was also confirmed by Holland, the fact that 'there are no pure professional types' (Holland, 1992).

4.1.3. The validity study of the 60 item version

The 120 item set of statement related to different occupational interests was too long, as respondents attested,[38] hence the *Inventario de las Preferencias Profesionales de los Jovenes (IPPJ)* questionnaire was edited to a shorter and

---

[38] Respondents during the pilot test frequently complained of the length of the questionnaire and repetition of items. This caused them to be bored while responding to items on the final part of the test.

more reliable version. The next stage of analysis aimed to analyze the validity of the final, 60-item version of the questionnaire.

The first step was to eliminate all items with factor loadings below .40 from the model matrix (Stevens, 1992). Considering exploratory Factor Analysis of all 120 items of the pilot version, 93 positions reached a value greater than .40 (between .408 to .826). Guadagnoli and Velicer (1988) mention the significant influence of the factor loadings value on the assessment of the reliability results. If certain factors consist of 4 (or more) items with a factor loading greater than .6, then such results should be considered reliable, regardless of the sample size. On the other hand, if the sample size is greater than 150, the analysis results should be considered to be reliable if each factor consists of 10 or more items and each item has a loading factor greater than .4. The conducted analysis gave statistical evidence that all scales fulfill this condition.

The total variance for a particular IPPJ item consists of two components: part of an item's variance is shared with other items (eg. other RIASEC subscales items) and it is called common variance, and part is specific to the measure of the one distinct subscale of the RIASEC model and is denoted unique variance. The concept of communality may be defined as the proportion of a variable's (or an item) variance explained by a factor structure.

Hence, the communality measure as the proportion of common variance within a variable (common variance) for the individual items had values between .339 and .792. This was confirmed by the analysis of the reconstructed correlation matrix, which is analyzed in the next step (the matrix indicated differences between the observed correlations and predicted coefficients for the model). It allowed the elimination of all items where the absolute measures of non-redundant components were higher than .05 (Field, 2005). There were 4% of such items in the analyzed matrix; thus no elimination of an excessive number of items was necessary, which allowed for the establishment of the final version of the *Inventario de las Preferencias Profesionales de los Jovenes (IPPJ)*.

A final version of the IPPJ questionnaire was created as a result of this analysis, and consists of 60 test items related to six RIASEC subscales. Each subscale consists of 10 items. The statements are listed in the RIASEC sequence, which means that every seventh item falls on a given scale. The Final IPPJ questionnaire is attached in the Appendix 5.

The next step of analysis undertaken on the 60-item version of the questionnaire was the test of internal structure, using Factor Analysis. Bartlett's test of sphericity was significant at $p<.0001$, $\chi2 = 34501.348$, and the value of KMO index was .921, which is classified as very high (Hutcheson and Sofroniou, 1999).

As a result of the Factor Analysis standardized with Promax rotation, 10 principal components were indicated with a value above 1. All these factors together explain 59.003% of the total variance. The scree plot (Figure 13.) indicates the existence of six major factors, which explain 51.03% of the total variance, while the rotation sums of squared loadings were for subsequent factors as follows: (1) 17.58%; (2) 11.12%; (3) 7.39%; (4) 6.97%; (5) 44.08% and (6) 3.88%.

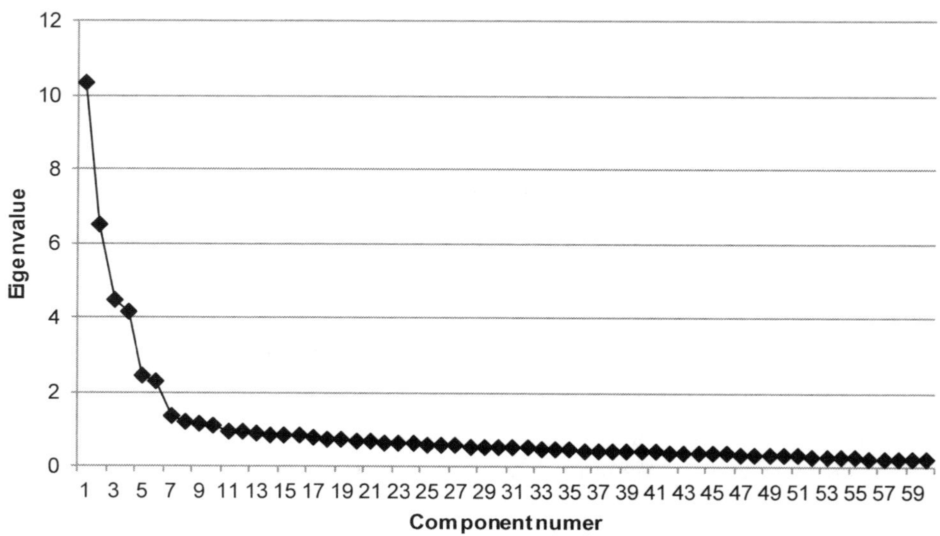

Figure 13. Scree plot of Factor Analysis with eigenvalues for factor numbers
in the 60 item version

The measure of commonality for individual items ranged from .38 to .77 (M = .59; SD = .09). MacCallum, Widaman, Zhang and Hong (1999) argue that commonality indicators play a key role in the assessment of the reliability of the results of the factor analysis, their replication and the representativeness of the population as well as in the indication of measures of error in the sample. The authors demonstrated that with the increase of the commonality statistics (especially above .50), the significance of the sample size decreases, which means that the replicability of results in the population will be high.

Analysis of the anti-image-correlation matrix presenting the individual measures of the KMO for each individual variable (values outside of the diagonal represent the partial correlation between variables and should be as small as possible) showed that the 60-item version of the questionnaire fulfills requirements of the KMO measure in respect to each distinct item. None of the items should have a value below .5 (Field, 2005). These measures for individual items ranged from .836 (item 42) to .963 (item 28). Factor loadings for 6 subscales with items in English are shown in table 12.

The items that were included in a certain factor are bolded (Table 12). The correlation analysis indicated that some interests' types are related. The factor representing Social interests is correlated with Artistic preferences (.391) and Enterprising (.348). Secondly, the Enterprising type coincides with Conventional preferences.

Table 12. Component matrix: Factor loadings for each position of the final version of the IPPJ after rotation

Items	Principal Component					
	Factor 1 (R)	Factor 2 (I)	Factor 3 (S)	Factor 4 (A)	Factor 5 (E)	Factor 6 (C)
1	2	3	4	5	6	7
55. I would like to design and mend machines and modern devices.	.823	.119				
7. I would like to work in the technical service of some company.	.808		.162			
49. I like learning how technical devices work.	.793					
13. I am interested in technical aspects of the automotive industry.	.778					
37. I would like to work in a car service station.	.777					−.148
25. In the future, I would like to work with tools and technical devices.	.734	,120				.134
1. I like making some small repairs of domestic equipment.	.702					
43. I would like to learn how to make technical drawings.	.564			.345	−.117	.114
19. Drawing schemes and group projects is a very nice and interesting task to me.	.542			.153	.103	
31. I know the way a computer is designed and the way it functions.	.499	.117	−.198			.101
38. I am interested in new branches of science, such as genetics and biotechnology.		.817	.137			
14. I like scientific discoveries and new inventions.		.797	−.175			
8. I would like to work in a research center or a laboratory.		.769	.127			
56. I am interested in new branches of science and technology.	.209	.764				
20. I like carrying out experiments and observing how they are carried out.		.755		.110		
50. I would like to study the brain functioning.	−.132	.754	.269			−.110
2. A conflictive job seems very interesting to me.		.728				
26. I like watching TV programs dedicated to scientific news.		.723	−.152			

Table 12. cont.

1	2	3	4	5	6	7
44. I would like to carry out research and discover the vaccine for a serious disease.		**.699**	.350			
32. When walking in the mountains or in a forest, I stop to take a closer look at plants and trees that are new to me.		**.306**	.285	.252	−.196	.136
46. In my future job I would like to help disabled people.		.178	**.772**		−.141	
34. In the future I would like to work with young boys and girls.			**.749**		−.108	
28. With pleasure and dedication I would teach teenagers about how to avoid some addictions.			**.748**			
4. I would like to take care of people with mental diseases.		.108	**.694**		−.190	
40. I would like to help people to solve their social problems.			**.671**		.271	
52. I would like to work in a telephone assistance center for teenagers.	.286	−.102	**.671**			
22. I would feel good helping people to understand each other.			**.626**		.141	.113
58. I would feel good at helping people who are nervous or sad for some reason.			**.625**		.155	
16. I like taking part in social works.	−.102		**.589**		.156	
10. I like participating in non-governmental organizations, such as the Red Cross or a scout movement.	−.153	.219	**.504**	.104		
39. I would like to create or compose some kind of music.	.104			**.798**		
33. I would like to play in a music band or an orchestra.				**.783**		−.107
21. I like taking part in art, music and literature classes.	−.147			**.780**	.115	
51. In the future, I would like to express myself through a creative activity, such as painting, drawing, sculpture, dancing or singing.			.180	**.758**		
3. I can play a musical instrument or I would like to learn how to do it.		.106	−.209	**.676**		.119

1	2	3	4	5	6	7
15. I would like to see school exhibits of sculpture, paintings and photographs.	−.100			**.631**		.131
9. In the future I would like to write poems, movie or games scripts.	.172			**.610**		−.146
57. I would like to act in performances: to dance, sing or interpret some roles.		−.163	.213	**.589**	.134	
27. I am interested in magazines about art, furniture and architecture.	.190			**.509**		
45. I would like to make drawings for book or create posters.	.175		.271	**.466**		
59. I like to control the work of other people.	.100		−.140		**.749**	
53. I would like to learn how to lead a group of people in order to control their actions.					**.707**	
17. In group activities I encourage leadership and coordination.	−.142		−.156		**.690**	.134
41. I would like to have the role of a class president.					**.663**	
23. I like having a word in different discussions and convincing people.				.142	**.621**	
35. I can give instructions and advice to other people.	−.109				**.564**	.143
5. It makes me feel good and I can manage the organization of my school mates' work, when I have to assign tasks to them and check out if they have been completed.		.125	−.104		**.542**	
47. I would like to have a job where I could make decisions and plan actions for other people.			.183	−.101	**.539**	
29. I would like to lead a group of my school mates in order to organize a school party		−.141	.210		**.515**	
11. Sometimes at school I solve conflicts between my mates.			.168		**.495**	
42. On my desk I like to have everything perfectly organized.					−.121	**.812**
54. I like to have my desk and my room well-organized.						**.809**

Table 12. cont.

1	2	3	4	5	6	7
6. I like to keep my notebooks clean and well-organized.	−.266			.110		**.686**
60. I like organizing my work every day and for the whole week.					.175	**.629**
24. I like respecting and meeting deadlines.		.107				**.625**
36. In the evenings, I like planning the work I have to do next day.					.149	**.542**
48. I like to plan and control adequately my expenses.	.182				.128	**.491**
30. I would like to have a calm job with clear rules or instructions.	.207		.169			**.481**
12. In my job I would like to work in accordance with some strictly defined rules.	.160		.116	−.176		**.465**
18. I would like to have a job where I could do some precise tasks.	.246			−.131		**.433**

Table 13. Matrix of correlations between factor analysis components of the 60 item IPPJ questionnaire final version

Principal components	1 (R)	2 (I)	3 (S)	4 (A)	5 (E)	6 (C)
1 (R)	1.00	.268	−.086	.153	.079	.159
2 (I)		1.00	.161	.126	.089	.213
3 (S)			1.00	**.391**	**.348**	.231
4 (A)				1.00	.224	.089
5 (E)					1.00	**.353**
6 (C)						1.00

Designation of load factors: R – Realistic, I – Innovative, A – Artistic, S – Social, E – Enterprising, C – Conventional

As both 120 and 60 item versions of the IPPJ have satisfying psychometric features both versions (see Appendix 4 and 5) may be applied in the diagnosis of vocational preferences, however the normalization was made only for the shortest 60-item version. The extended version will be especially useful in the future updating of the questionnaire, e.g., every 10 years, according to rapid socio-cultural and labor market changes to better adapt the tool to the constantly evolving concept of vocational personality and the job and occupation-like designates of RIASEC vocational types.

Summing up, the results of the orthogonal rotation, where all factors remain uncorrelated with one another, are only a partly adequate statistical solution. They are in line with the nature of professional preferences, that though there are independent interests' types, however the construct of professional personality implies complexity, where there is more than one vocational interest, and interests may be interrelated (Table 13).

4.1.4. Confirmatory Factor Analysis

To test the hypothesis that the model fits the data, Confirmatory Factor Analysis (CFA) was carried out, whose results are summarized in Figure 14. To perform the CFA IBM SPSS Amos (Version 24) was used (Maximum Likelihood). Based on Hoyle's (2011) recommendations, and according to the multi-faceted approach to the assessment of model fit the following goodness of fit indices were considered: (a) χ^2 likelihood ratio statistic, (b) comparative fit index (CFI), (c) root mean square error of approximation (RMSEA), (d) the Tucker-Lewis index (TLI), (e) standardized root mean residual (SRMR), and (f) HOLTER fit index. A statistically insignificant χ^2 suggests good fit, but χ^2 is biased by large sample sizes, such as those in this study. CFI is less dependent on sample size, and values greater than .90 indicate an acceptable model fit (Hu & Bentler, 1995). Values of RMSEA equal to or less than .06 indicate a good fit (Hu & Bentler, 1999), but the RMSEA ignores the complexity of a model (i.e., a large number of estimated parameters) as is the case for the model tested in this study (60 observed variables, 6 factors). Additional support for the fit of the solution would be evidence by a 90% interval of the RMSEA whose upper limit is below cutoff values (e.g. .08) (MacCallum, Brown & Sugawara, 1996). TLI incorporates a correction for model complexity, and values greater than .90 indicate an acceptable fit (Bentler & Bonett, 1980). The SRMR has also no penalty for model complexity and values of the SRMR less than .08 are generally considered favorable (Kline, 2005). HOELTER (Hu & Bentler, 1998) index states the sample size at which chi square would not be significant (alpha = .05), i.e., that is how small one's sample size would have to be for the result to be no longer significant. HOELTER values higher than 200 indicate good model fit.

Confirmatory Factor Analysis showed that model is reasonably consistent with the data. Fit indexes were acceptable but to varying degrees: $\chi^2 = 11203.44$, $df = 1695$ (but large N solutions are routinely rejected on the basis of χ^2), CFI = .80 (the CFI, and the TLI which follows, depends on the average size of the correlations in the data. If the average correlation between variables are not high – as is the case with the factors in the model – then the CFI and TLI will not be very high); RMSEA = .060, for a 90% CI = .059, .061), TLI = 0.77., SRMR = .07, HOELTER = 250.

Although model evaluation usually brings with the examination of fit indices, it is equally important (Brown, 2006) to examine solution in terms of potential areas of localized strains and the interpretability and strength of resulting parameter estimates. With this caveats in mind in this model all factor loadings were calculated and they appeared substantial and significant (z values [1.96]). Average loadings for items in each factor are high: Realistic (M = .68), Investigative (M =.69), Artistic (M = .64), Social (M = .66), Enterprising (M = .57), and Conventional (M = .56). Correlations between subscales ranged from −.06 to .48 (M = .24, SD = 0.16). No correlated errors were found, so the subscales are one-dimensional, because there was no shared variance.

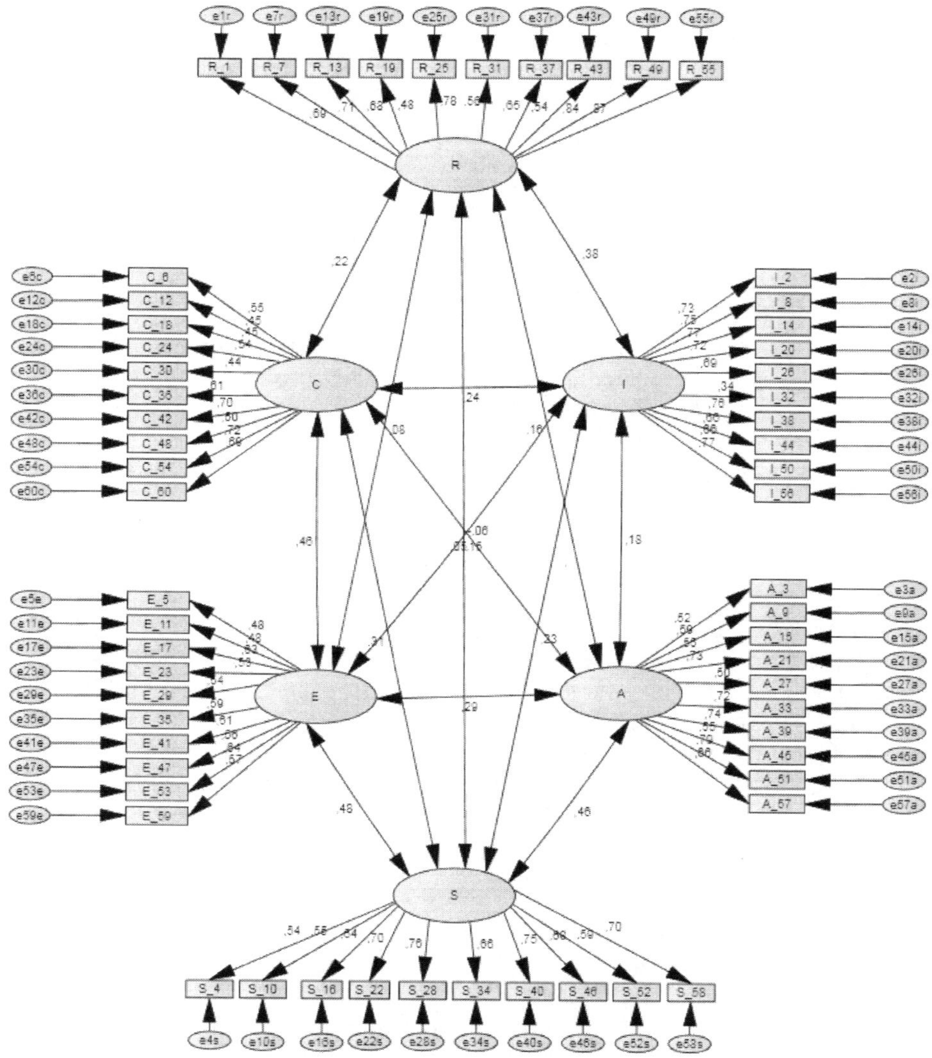

Figure 14. Final model of factorial structure for the Inventory of the Occupational Preferences of Youth (standardized estimates)

4.1.5. The reliability of the IPPJ scale

Validity is a necessary but insufficient condition in psychological measurement. Reliability analysis was the next phase of the tool construction, after six scales were indicated in the exploratory Factor Analysis. The objective of this study was to characterize statistical features of the items associated to each of the 6 RIASEC subscales, and especially their relation to the general test purpose and objective. The aim of the reliability study was to estimate the ability of the IPPJ test to produce consistent results when occupational interests were measured under different conditions such as during the test-retest or in case of the repeated items in the IPPJ.

To be valid, the psychometric tool must first be reliable and to achieve psychometric evidence for the quality of the IPPJ, three techniques of reliability testing were planned:

(1) The Internal Consistency Reliability test;

(2) Internal reliability test ("lay test" by repeating 6 items in the pilot study).

(3) Test-Retest Reliability;

The Internal Consistency Reliability procedure is based on the correlations between different items of subscales (in our case 6 RIASEC scales) and the entire IPPJ test. Other words, it measures whether the set of items (e.g. 10 items of one of RIASEC scale types) that intend to measure the same general construct (specific occupational interest) produces similar scores. The internal consistency measures to what extend each item is an indicator of the aspects measured by the whole test. It measures whether "the test is a pure measure of the distinct variable (vocational type) and the extent to which the answers to an individual item measure the same thing throughout the test result" (Brzeziński, 2006; Field, 2005).

In case of response scales such as in the IPPJ, where respondents choose one of several responses to the items presented (I do not agree, rather disagree, it is difficult to say, rather agree, I completely agree), it is recommended that reliability indicators should be established by the Cronbach's alpha coefficient for scales and positions, according to the Cronbach's recommendations (1951).

Cronbach's alpha, (α) test is the most common measure of scale reliability. It is related to other and more basic split-half reliability tests as it is based on computing the correlation coefficient for each split, and the average of these values is equivalent to Cronbach's alpha (Field, 2005).

Another statistic that was calculated for each item was the discriminative power indicator, which indicates the extent to which the study population is differentiated in terms of a specific, relevant feature. It is expressed by the correlation coefficient between the item and the overall result of a scale. The higher the value of this indicator, the higher the discriminatory power of the item. A low value (less than 0.3) may mean that the given position measures some other aspects than the scale as a whole.

The next parameter that was calculated was the reliability coefficient of each item. Item reliability indicates how the item contributes to total score variance, where higher values represent better reliability. This factor is a function of the variance of each test position and the marker of the correlation between the item and the overall result of the test. Operationally it is expressed as the product of the standard deviation and the correlation of the item and the test. This indicator allowed items to be determined according to the degree of differentiation with regard to the measured feature (occupational preferences). This is because this indicator takes into account the item variance, which significantly influences the relative contribution to the overall reliability of the tasks in the entire test. It is especially useful when two tasks have the same discriminatory power (the same correlation between the task and the test). In this case, the task with a greater variance will increase the reliability of the whole test (see Crocker and Algina, 1986).

Other statistical measures determined include the mean and Standard Deviations (SD) to quantify the amount of variation for the scale and Standard Error of Measurement (SEM), which is a function of the reliability of the test and the dispersion of results (Guilford, 2005). Information about the Standard Error of Measurement is required to determine the confidence interval (CI) for the particular result of a tested individual. The choice of the confidence interval for the interpretation of the result condition the risk level of the investigator who exposes themselves to the fact that the young person's result may be outside of the acceptable range. Davis (1964) states that for the realities of professional career guidance it is necessary to accept a confidence interval (CI) around 85% (85% CI = X ± 1,44 SEM). The risk of error in that case is not greater than 15 cases out of 100. In the present statistical analysis of IPPJ, however, a level of CI as 95% was accepted as a valid confidence interval (95% CI = X ± 1,96 SEM). The results obtained for each of 6 scales are presented in tables from 14 to 19.

Table 14. Properties of individual items and the reliability measures of the scale of Realistic Interests, N = 1317

Item	M	SD	α-Cronbach after removal of the item	The indicator of the discriminative power of the item	Item reliability indicator
P7	2.93	1.316	.887	.778	.889
P49	3.33	1.309	.880	.661	.809
P13	2.84	1.342	.888	.723	.887
P25	3.42	1.312	.883	.630	.948
P37	2.36	1.284	.890	.644	.809
P1	2.79	1.320	.889	.539	.851
P43	3.12	1.340	.896	.489	.722
P19	3.19	1.205	.898	.511	.590
P31	3.41	1.164	.897	.806	.595
P55	3.04	1.368	.877	.778	.889

M for the scale = 3.44
SD for the scale = 9.38
α-Cronbach for the Realistic Interests Scale = .899
SEM = 2.98
85% CI = 4.21
95% CI = 5.84

Table 15. Properties of individual items and the reliability measures
of the scale of Investigative Interests, N = 1317

Item	M	SD	α-Cronbach after removal of the item	The indicator of the discriminative power of the item	Item reliability indicator
P38	3.24	1.324	.886	.749	.991
P50	3.22	1.304	.892	.659	.860
P8	3.47	1.266	.888	.717	.908
P56	3.62	1.183	.888	.722	.854
P14	3.80	1.146	.889	.716	.820
P44	3.30	1.322	.892	.664	.878
P20	3.77	1.116	.891	.682	.762
P26	3.59	1.186	.893	.645	.765
P2	3.88	1.111	.891	.680	.755
P32	3.79	1.194	.912	.334	.399

M for the scale = 35.67
SD for the scale = 8.88
α-Cronbach for the Investigative Interests Scale = .902
SEM = 2.78
85% CI = 4.00
95% CI = 5.44

Table 16. Properties of individual items and the reliability measures
of the scale of Artistic Interests, N = 1317

Item	M	SD	α-Cronbach after removal of the item	The indicator of the discriminative power of the item	Item reliability indicator
P51	2.90	1.385	.847	.742	.961
P21	3.18	1.288	.852	.687	.885
P39	3.00	1.412	.851	.691	.976
P33	2.72	1.384	.853	.663	.918
P57	2.60	1.455	.861	.577	.839
P15	3.64	1.183	.864	.529	.626
P3	3.89	1.193	.867	.483	.576
P9	2.85	1.307	.863	.544	.711
P27	2.96	1.248	.868	.476	.594
P45	2.71	1.263	.866	.502	.635

M for the scale = 3.45
SD for the scale i = 8.95
α-Cronbach for the Artistic Interests Scale = .872
SEM = 3.20
85% CI = 4.61
95% CI = 6.27

Table 17. Properties of individual items and the reliability measures
of the scale of Social Interests, N = 1317

Item	M	SD	α-Cronbach after removal of the item	The indicator of the discriminative power of the item	Item reliability indicator
P34	2.79	1.263	.875	.643	.812
P46	3.25	1.246	.874	.667	.831
P28	3.45	1.273	.870	.706	.899
P52	2.60	1.196	.882	.547	.654
P40	3.28	1.160	.871	.701	.812
P22	3.73	1.110	.875	.649	.720
P58	3.70	1.153	.875	.647	.746
P16	3.37	1.111	.877	.620	.688
P10	3.10	1.266	.884	.528	.668
P4	2.82	1.179	.883	.532	.628

M for the scale = 32.09
SD for the scale = 8.44
α-Cronbach for the Social Interests Scale = .888
SEM = 2.82
85% CI = 4.06
95% CI = 5.53

Table 18. Properties of individual items and the reliability measures
of the scale of Enterprising Interests, N = 1317

Item	M	SD	α-Cronbach after removal of the item	The indicator of the discriminative power of the item	Item reliability indicator
P17.	3.68	.981	.796	.579	.335
P59.	3.42	1.102	.801	.528	.278
P23	3.66	1.092	.806	.485	.235
P53	3.46	1.054	.796	.574	.330
P29	3.80	.951	.809	.446	.199
P41	2.84	1.330	.803	.524	.275
P35	3.90	.918	.802	.524	.274
P11	3.38	1.039	.811	.433	.187
P5	3.61	1.063	.808	.457	.209
P47.	3.79	1.011	.804	.497	.247

M for the scale = 35.39
SD for the scale = 6.89
α-Cronbach for the Enterprising Interests Scale = .820
SEM = 2.92
85% CI = 4.20
95% CI = 5.72

Table 19. Properties of individual items and the reliability measures
of the scale of Conventional Interests, N = 1317

Item	M	SD	α-Cronbach after removal of the item	The indicator of the discriminative power of the item	Item reliability indicator
P42	4.10	.982	.792	.604	.525
P54	4.13	.965	.790	.630	.530
P6	4.51	.719	.811	.425	.189
P24	4.15	.878	.804	.501	.237
P60	3.69	1.026	.792	.607	.505
P30	4.22	1.020	.810	.435	.218
P12	3.53	1.203	.812	.443	.308
P48	4.22	.882	.808	.452	.191
P18	3.78	1.047	.809	.449	.274
P36	3.63	1.085	.802	.513	.452

M for the scale = 4.40
SD for the scale = 6.07
α-Cronbach for the Conventional Interests Scale = .823
SEM = 2.55
85% CI = 3.67
95% CI = 5.00

All α-Cronbach coefficients for the six IPPJ scales were higher than .80. This indicates that each of the scales is a homogeneous construct with high internal consistency. Correlations between distinct items of the corresponding scale (of the RIASEC set) indicate a high discriminative power factor for each of IPPJ hexagon scales. Correlation values range from .334 (the only item with the lowest indicator of 10 items of Investigative scale) to items with a correlation of .806.

4.1.6. Internal reliability scale: Duplicated items in "Lay key"

The final technique applied in the IPPJ questionnaire revision was the control scale, which measures the reliability of answers by checking whether the respondent answers the same way to the same questions, or whether their responses are by chance or intentionally adulterated. This scale differs from the traditional way of measuring reliability used in cases when, for example, job candidates cheat when filling out personality questionnaires – the most frequently used procedures in such cases are social desirability tests.

Because of the difficulty in applying two equivalent versions of the test for the vocational interest's assessment according to Holland's model, an alternative technique was applied to check internal consistency of the tool by estimating the degree to which multiple measures of the same item agree with one another. We checked the parallel-items reliability comparing scores for the same item in the IPPJ.

In the total 126 items version, 6 items were randomly selected, 1 item from each of 6 RIASEC scales and repeated to see the reliability of replies to these 6 items. Item numbers for each Interest type were: A_121; E_122; I_123; C_124; R_125; S_126 (see Appendix 1). The correlation between repeated items is presented in Table 20.

Table 20. Correlation coefficients for the repeated items:
A_121; D_122; I_123; M_124; R_125; S_126[39]

Correlations		A_121	E_122	I_123	C_124	R_125	S_126
A_31	Pearson Correlation	.733**	.190**	.174**	.010	−.011	.113**
	N	1556	1543	1548	1553	1555	1553
E_32	Pearson Correlation	.101**	.678**	.258**	.153**	−.020	.145**
	N	1548	1536	1539	1545	1546	1544
I_33	Pearson Correlation	.073**	.271**	.615**	.212**	.012	.145**
	N	1551	1540	1545	1548	1552	1548
C_34	Pearson Correlation	−.054*	.193**	.216**	.629**	.154**	.201**
	N	1552	1540	1544	1549	1551	1549
R_35	Pearson Correlation	.023	.027	−.004	.197**	.789**	−.023
	N	1553	1542	1547	1550	1554	1550
S_36	Pearson Correlation	.037	.096**	.152**	.230**	−.056*	.704**
	N	1551	1538	1543	1548	1550	1549

Significance level (two sided): * $p < .05$; **$p < .01$

The procedure to check insincerity of respondents in the IPPJ was a simple *lie scale* created by 6 items.[40] In the significant number of all 120 items to operationalize different types of occupational interests, the person was asked to

---

[39] See the items from the 120 item version in Appendix 1:
A_Me gusta participar en de clases arte, de música o de literatura.
E_En las actividades de grupo fomento el liderazgo y la coordinación.
I_Me gusta pensar en las causas y consecuencias de los acontecimientos.
C_Me gustaría tener un trabajo donde tenga que realizar tareas muy precisas.
R_Me interesan los aspectos técnicos de la industria automovilística.
S_Me sentiría bien en un trabajo que requiriera de mí mucha paciencia y comprensión frente a los demás.
[40] All literal duplicates were excluded in other statistical analysis (eg. EFA).

answer twice for identical items. The reliability was represented by the correlation of the scores in the literally repeated items in a single administration of the IPPJ (Anastasi, & Urbina, 1997).

The analysis of correlation between pairs of repeated answers was applied in the extended 120 pilot test. Summing up, all correlation measures (Table 20) indicate high correlation between pairs of repeated answers. Pearson's (r) correlation coefficient range from .615 to .789. Results of this additional procedure confirm the high reliability of the tool and items that compose the IPPJ based on the regularity of responses of youth taking the IPPJ test.

4.1.7. Reliability as test-retest stability of the IPPJ scores

An important psychometric characteristic of the tool is its reliability in terms of results stability checked by analyzing the results obtained by the respondents in a repeated test. To measure test-retest reliability, the same version of the IPPJ test was administered twice on the same sample of high school students, at two different times. This method of reliability testing is based on the assumption that there is no significant or relatively low change (Holland, 1997) in the professional interest measurement between the test and retest of the same group of persons. The time interval is a significant aspect of this measure as the correlation between the two observations, among many factors, depends on the time that elapses between the test and the retest, which means that the shorter the gap, the higher the expected correlation.

Stability of the results was determined by comparing the results of two measurements made on the same group with a certain interval (in this case it was 5 weeks). The estimated reliability indicator obtained by this method was the coefficient of absolute stability. This measure 'indicates the extent to which the test results are sensitive to random influence and changes, related to both the subject and test conditions' (Hornowska, 2007, p. 49). In accordance with the recommendation of Nowakowska (1975), this test should not be the only method of estimating reliability and therefore the retest was used as one of several techniques to check the IPPJ reliability.

In order to assess the indicator of absolute stability of test results a group of 295 students randomly selected from the total number of 1317 students was investigated, taking into account a good representation of girls and boys (Table 21). The retest group of students represented most of Ecuador's 24 provinces. From among the total number of 295 students, 253 respondents were from urban and 42 from rural areas. The average age of the selected group ranged from 16 to 20 years (M = 16.98, SD = .90). The test was repeated 5 weeks after the first test and conducted with the same testing procedure to determine absolute test stability. Table 21 shows the structure of this group by gender and education profile in the secondary school. Tables 22 and 23 indicate other characteristics of the retest sample (school profile and number of students from each school).

Table 21. The characteristic of the retest sample in regard to gender and educational profile of the trial version of the pilot IPPJ questionnaire

Gender	School profile				Total	
	technical		general			
	N	%	N	%	N	%
Girls	4	1.4	125	42.5	127	56.2
Boys	8	2.7	158	21.2	162	43.8
Total	12	4.1	283	95.9	295	100

The 120 items version of the questionnaire was applied in the retest. It was carried out in eight secondary schools, both public and private, and consisted of the two school profiles: general and technical education schools, they being the largest and most representative ones (Table 22).

Table 22. School profile structure of the sample of students included in the retest of the trial version of the pilot IPPJ questionnaire

Institution	School code	Status	Province
Unidad Educativa La Concordia	1	Fiscal	Pichincha
Unidad Educativa José María Velaz	2	Fiscomisional	Pichincha
Colegio Juan Pio Montúfar	3	Fiscal	Pichincha
Colegio Sagrados Corazones de Rumipamba	4	Particular	Pichincha
Colegio Militar Eloy Alfaro	5	Fiscomisional	Pichincha
Unidad Educativa Nanegalito	6	Fiscal	Pichincha
Spellman	7	Particular	Pichincha
Unidad Educativa Municipal San Francisco de Quito	8	Municipal	Pichincha

Table 23. The number of randomly selected students included in the retest in each of schools of the trial version of the pilot IPPJ questionnaire

Institution	Status	Province	Number of students
Unidad Educativa La Concordia	Fiscal	Pichincha	42
Unidad Educativa José María Velaz	Fiscomisional	Pichincha	11
Colegio Juan Pio Montúfar	Fiscal	Pichincha	78
Colegio Sagrados Corazones de Rumipamba	Particular	Pichincha	27
Colegio Militar Eloy Alfaro	Fiscomisional	Pichincha	66
Unidad Educativa Nanegalito	Fiscal	Pichincha	14
Spellman	Particular	Pichincha	39
Unidad Educativa Municipal San Francisco de Quito	Municipal	Pichincha	18
Total:			295

Results obtained in the first test were correlated with the results in the second round test. Table 24 presents bolded results that refer to the 120 items and also indicates the correlation indicators for 60 items of the final version of the IPPJ. The retest also served as an additional criterion in analysis of the most stable items, so that the least reliable items in terms of their low retest results stability were excluded from the pilot version. Hence all 120 items are presented.

The correlation measures were calculated by the Pearson product-moment correlation to establish the measure of the linear correlation between the test and retest result. All covariance measures ranged from .416 to .796, especially considering the 60 items selected from the 120-item pilot version for the final version of the IPPJ.

It is significant that even in the pilot version almost all of the 120 coefficients obtained values higher than .30 (Table 24) and are statistically significant at the .01 level. It justifies the full 120 item version as an acceptable tool for the vocational interests study.

Table 24. Results stability for IPPJ items in the pilot version of the IPPJ (120 items)

Item	r	Item	r	Item	r
1	2	3	4	5	6
1.	.607**	41.	.620**	81.	**.702***
2.	.535**	42.	**.661***	82.	.640**
3.	.693**	43.	.562**	83.	.512**
4.	**.424***	44.	**.477***	84.	.440**
5.	.464**	45.	**.557***	85.	**.631***
6.	**.631***	46.	.588**	86.	.713**
7.	.635**	47.	**.492***	87.	**.585***
8.	.356**	48.	**.517***	88.	.586**
9.	.580**	49.	**.630***	89.	**.707***
10.	.408**	50.	**.664***	90.	**.796***
11.	.636**	51.	**.498***	91.	.361**
12.	**.550***	52.	.641**	92.	.704**
13.	**.653***	53.	**.632***	93.	**.754***
14.	**.416***	54.	.757**	94.	.379**
15.	.403**	55.	.670**	95.	.492**
16.	.509**	56.	**.520***	96.	**.511***
17.	**.681***	57.	.683**	97.	**.704***
18.	.535**	58.	.461**	98.	**.566***
19.	**.678***	59.	**.652***	99.	**.697***
20.	**.605***	60.	.714**	100.	**.643***
21.	.526**	61.	.701**	101.	**.586***
22.	.435**	62.	.302**	102.	**.731***
23.	**.708***	63.	.702**	103.	**.630***

Table 24. cont.

1	2	3	4	5	6
24.	.663**	64.	.677**	104.	.573**
25.	.598**	65.	.656**	105.	.757**
26.	.453**	66.	.740**	106.	.579**
27.	.541**	67.	.621**	107.	.583**
28.	.643**	68.	.596**	108.	.764**
29.	.459**	69.	.621**	109.	.665**
30.	.454**	70.	.631**	110.	.529**
31.	.700**	71.	.577**	111.	.678**
32.	.578**	72.	.761**	112.	.580**
33.	.425**	73.	.693**	113.	.498**
34.	.603**	74.	.452**	114.	.757**
35.	.718**	75.	.696**	115.	.711**
36.	.513**	76.	.601**	116.	.656**
37.	.456**	77.	.584**	117.	.546**
38.	.567**	78.	.808**	118.	.442**
39.	.456**	79.	.601**	119.	.593**
40.	.482**	80.	.622**	120.	.569**

Significance level: **–$p < .01$

As shown in Table 25, the level of stability of the results of the IPPJ questionnaire for the 60-item version of the RIASEC test in all 6 subscales can be regarded as high. The most stable results were achieved by students in regard to the scale of Realistic Interests, with a high r-Pearson coefficient .881. This result signifies that this kind of interest in the tested group of students (16–19 years old) is relatively constant in comparison to 5 other types of preferences. The lowest result value, while still regarded as generally high, is $r = .757$ for the Enterprising Interest scale. This case may imply that these types of preferences may be still crystallizing and are expressed by a greater variation over time, or that the stability of items related to the Enterprising Interest subscale is lower than other ones.

Table 25. Results stability for six subscales of the IPPJ pilot questionnaire (60 items)

IPPJ Scale	r-Pearson coefficient
Realistic interests	.881**
Investigative interests	.762**
Artistic interests	.855**
Social interests	.819**
Enterprising interests	.757**
Conventional interests	.785**

Significance level **–$p < .01$

One important psychometric aspect of the research is whether the results are reliable and consistent. Stability results were also verified by the split half correlation method. This identifies reliability by the calculation of the correlation coefficient between scores on two halves of a test, which results in the average Inter-item Correlation.

Using this method, the test results were divided into half, where one half were results of the first run of the test and the second half were results of the retest, and were correlated (Ferguson, Takane, 1999). In the case of the stability testing of the IPPJ, the results of the first study with the results of the retest were satisfying, according to Guttman and Sperman-Brown indicators. Hence, both the Guttman (.846) and the Spearman-Brown (.847) test scores indicate that the results achieved in the first and the second study are characterized by high stability. The psychometric value of the IPPJ tools is also confirmed by a satisfactory score of the split half correlation coefficient, which is .734.

4.1.8. Construct validity study through the analysis of intergroup differences

The construct validity of the test may be indirectly confirmed in the analysis of what extent the test results "behave" like the theory suggests regarding the construct of professional personality. Empirical evidence related to gender differences claims that Holland's RIASEC model subscales differentiate males and females (Paessler, 2015; Paszkowska-Rogacz, 2011). Hence construct validity is also reflected in the result structure of distinct groups in regard to study of differences in vocational interests.

In order to check whether there are statistically significant differences in distinguished comparative groups, results were compared in all 6 scales between girls and boys, and additionally between place of student residence (rural and urban). At first, all research data were tested in terms of required assumptions and conditions for conducting parametric tests, for both versions: the longer IPPJ-120 and the shorter IPPJ-60. The normalization procedure was conducted only for the IPPJ-60, however.

We used ANOVA to determine whether there are any significant differences between the means in all RIASEC subscales' means in the group of girls and boys and between students with place of residence in rural and urban area. As the ANOVA is a parametric test and is based on normal distribution, this assumption was checked for using the Kolmogorov-Smirnov (K-S) test. The K-S test allows for the determination whether a sample comes from a population with a specific distribution and whether the distribution is normal or skewed. K-S test determines whether two data sets differ significantly. K-S indicators proved to be insignificant at all scales.

The assumption of equality of covariance matrices was also checked to fulfill all ANOVA test requirements. To tests the equality of variances between groups the Levene's test was applied and confirmed that most of the variance in the majority of compared groups is homogeneous.

After fulfilling these preliminary conditions, two-factor analysis of variance was conducted (the gender and type of school). Because no interaction effect was indicated between gender variable and school type, one-way analysis (ANOVA) was conducted separately for gender and place of residence. Results of this analysis are presented in Tables 26, 27 and 28 for the variable of gender, place of residence and school type.

Table 26. Results of ANOVA for girls and boys for 6 RIASEC scales
(IPPJ – 60 questionnaire)

Scale	Gender				F	Effect size $\eta2$
	Girls N = 962		Boys N = 970			
	M	SD	M	SD		
R	33.24	8.09	38.64	6.37	265.33***	.120
I	36.59	7.76	36.35	7.67	0.45	.000
A	35.07	7.52	34.57	7.57	2.14	.001
S	37.05	6.72	35.50	6.73	25.76***	.013
E	35.67	6.08	35.28	6.22	.16	.001
C	40.61	5.97	40.01	6.08	4.87*	.003

The level of significance: * p <.05; *** p <.001; R – Realistic interests, I – Investigative interests, A – Artistic interests, S – Social interests, E – Enterprising interests, C – Conventional interests

In the comparison of girls and boys completing secondary school the statistical difference was significant in three scales: Realistic, Social and Conventional, and was not significant in the scales of Investigative, Artistic and Enterprising (Table 26, Figure 15).

In one scale boys obtained statistically higher results (Realistic) and girls received higher scores in the Social and Conventional Interests subscales. Interestingly, in regard to the two scales of Realistic and Social preferences they explain meaningful percent of variance which is analogically 12.1% and 1.3%. Results are in the line with other empirical studies where similar relations were indicated (Paessler, 2015).

Generally students attending secondary schools with a technical profile have a higher intensity of occupational interest in Realistic scale which may imply more crystallized and stronger interests than their colleagues from the general profile schools (Table 27). Students from general profile schools present higher results in Investigative, Artistic and Social scales. Due to the big difference between the quantity of students in two groups (Technical profile – 566 and General profile – 1336), however, this effect is not very significant and rather indicates a tendency than a distinct rule.

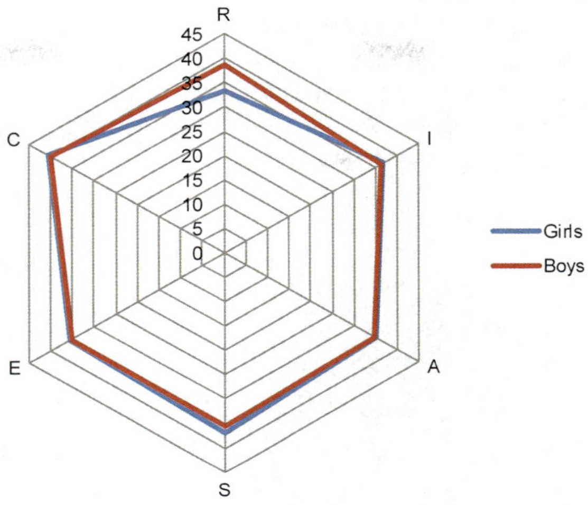

Figure 15. The diagram of mean scores for girls and boys in the final version of the IPPJ for RIASEC scales; Designation of load factors: R – Realistic, I – Innovative, A – Artistic, S – Social, E – Enterprising, C – Conventional

Table 27. Results of ANOVA for technical and general profile classes of the secondary schools for 6 RIASEC scales (IPPJ-60 questionnaire)

Scale	School profile					F	Effect size η2
	Technical profile N = 566		General profile N = 1336				
	M	SD	M	SD			
R	36.64	7.23	35.65	7.97		6.41**	.003
I	35.75	7.90	36.75	7.62		6.77**	.004
A	34.10	7.81	35.13	7.39		7.49**	.004
S	35.66	7.11	36.53	6.59		6.66**	.003
E	35.31	6.08	35.55	6.20		0.71	.000
C	40.51	5.76	40.26	6.11		0.62	.000

The level of significance: ** $p < .01$; Designation of load factors: R – Realistic, I – Innovative, A – Artistic, S – Social, E – Enterprising, C – Conventional

The greatest and statistically significant differences refer to higher scores for technical school students in R, A, S, C scales (Table 27). This might suggest that persons completing education in the technical profile have the strongest interests characterized especially by Conventional, Social and Realistic preferences (Figure16). Additionally, the lowest scores in the Artistic scale for both school profiles, particularly general profile classes are notable. The scores of the two groups of students (technical and general school profile) might imply an impact of specific variables related to the crystallization of youth interests and differentiation level of occupational identity demonstrated by the influence of the education system and the school type. However these findings require more deep and systematic research and analysis.

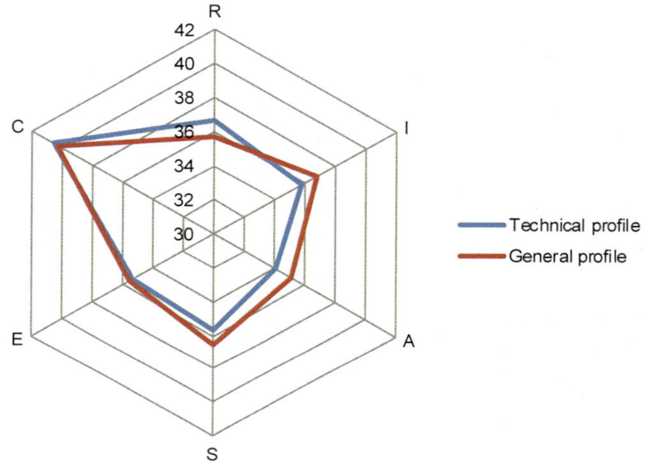

Figure 16. The diagram of mean scores for technical and general profile secondary school classes for 6 scales; Designation of load factors: R – Realistic, I – Innovative, A – Artistic, S – Social, E – Enterprising, C – Conventional

Table 28. Results of ANOVA between students living in rural and urban areas for 6 scales (IPPJ-60 questionnaire)

Scale	Place of residence				F	Effect size $\eta 2$
	Rural N = 305		Urban N = 938			
	M	SD	M	SD		
R	36.65	7.36	34.75	8.26	26.37***	.014
I	36.43	7.51	36.52	8.06	.05	.000
A	35.14	7.38	34.14	7.78	7.62**	.004
S	36.33	6.62	36.12	7.08	0.42	.000
E	35.41	6.13	35.60	6.21	0.43	.000
C	40.63	5.70	39.77	6.57	8.69**	.005

The level of significance: ** p <.01; *** p <.001; R – Realistic interests. I – Investigative interests. A – Artistic interests. S – Social interests. E – Enterprising interests. C – Conventional interests

Another analysis showed statistically significant differences between the group of students living in rural and urban areas (Figure 17). There were significant differences in the Realistic scale, the Artistic scale, and the Conventional scale with regard to the place of residence (Table 28). Students from rural areas were characterized by significantly higher values in R, A, C scales. It may imply the residence in the rural area impacts on the strength of vocational interests, and may be associated with more opportunities and experience related to know occupations typical for Realistic, Artistic, and Conventional-like jobs and activities than their colleagues from the urban area. The differences in 3 scales of RIASEC model interests imply that the urban environment does not necessarily stimulate the development and clarification of occupational interests of students. However this relation requires more study to explain the impact of the region on the profile of youth interests in Ecuador.

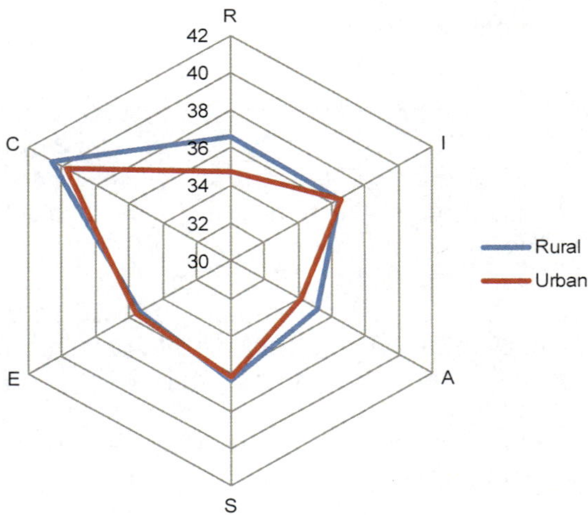

Figure 17. The diagram of mean scores for students leaving in rural and urban area for 6 scales; Designation of load factors: R – Realistic, I – Innovative, A – Artistic, S – Social, E – Enterprising, C – Conventional

Statistical analysis indicates significant differences in regard to gender, profile of the education but also between students from urban and rural areas (Table 26–28) and it may imply the construct validity of the psychometric instrument created to differentiate vocational interests of youth in Ecuador. All indicated relations may have a practical aspect for the vocational counseling process considering the effects of gender, residence and education profile. For practical reasons, not to exceed the number of variables considered for results interpretation, the norms were elaborated separately only for boys and girls in regard with indicated differences in the RIASEC subscales (see Appendices 10–14 with relevant norms).

4.1.9. Degree of differentiation and intensity of interest

The theoretical assumptions of Holland's model allow us to assess the degree of differentiation of personality profiles according to indicators developed by Holland and Iachan, where:

a) The differentiation index by Holland is determined by subtracting the lowest profile result from the highest;

b) L (Iachan's) differentiation index is calculated according to the following mathematical formula (mentioned also in the Chapter 3.2.3.):

$$L_1 = 1/2 \, [X_1 - (X_2 + X_4)/2]$$

where:
x_1 = highest profile score;
x_2 = the second highest profile score; and
x_4 = the fourth highest profile score.

The intensity of occupational interests was assessed by a simple measure (called also *elevation* – Hirschi, 2007), the sum of all six results in each of RIASEC scales (IPPJ-60), adding all the results of distinct scales. It turns out that this indicator is positively correlated with the stability of interest and maturity for a career (Fuller, Holland, & Johnston, 1999). Comparing coefficients of differentiation for girls and boys (Table 29), one may see a greater diversity of interests of girls and students of urban areas (Table 30) as well as technical schools (Table 30). Analysis of the intensity of interest shows slightly higher scores of boys and students from urban areas (Table 29 and 30).

Table 29. Iachan's and Holland's indicators of differentiation and intensity indicators for girls and boys, IPPJ-60 questionnaire

Indicator	Gender				F	Effect size $\eta2$
	Girls N = 962		Boys N = 970			
	M	SD	M	SD		
Lachan's indicator	2.85	1.77	2.40	1.58	34.93***	.017
Holland's indicator	14.45	6.75	12.42	6.05	48.54***	.012
Intensity indicator	218.24	29.14	22.35	31.14	2.36	.001

The level of significance: * p <.05; ** p <.01; *** p <.001

Table 30. Iachan's and Holland's indicators of differentiation and intensity indicators IPPJ for students from rural and urban areas, IPPJ-60 questionnaire

Indicator	Place of residence				F	Effect size η2
	Rural area N = 673		Urban area N = 1216			
	M	SD	M	SD		
Iachan's indicator	2.56	1.82	2.75	1.82	6.48*	.003
Holland's indicator	13.12	6.16	14.06	7.00	9.17**	.004
Intensity indicator	22.59	29.50	216.90	31.15	5.19*	.003

The level of significance: * p <.05; ** p <.01; *** p <.001

Indicators of post hoc analysis results (T2 Tamhane's test) with symbols of distinct subgroups differ at least at a level of p <.05.

Table 31. Iachan's and Holland's indicators of differentiation and intensity indicators for students from technical and general profile schools, IPPJ-60 questionnaire

Indicator	Class type				F	Effect size η2
	Technical class N = 566		General profile class N = 1336			
	M	SD	M	SD		
Iachan's indicator	2.76	1.80	2.57	1.63	5.10*	.003
Holland's indicator	13.90	6.60	13.21	6.45	4.40*	.000
Intensity indicator	217.97	29.60	219.88	3.39	1.60	.000

In the Appendix 11, 12, and 13 there are tables of standard norms of the differentiation and intensity indicators created for girls and boys. The intensity and diversity indicators have been developed separately for boys and girls in accordance with the results of the discriminative analysis.

5. Normalization procedure and analysis

The aim of this final phase of the development of the IPPJ was to elaborate reference standards for the raw results of the six vocational interests' scales and relate them to the standardization sample to determine the location of the respondent in the overall statistical range.

What is normalization and why is it needed? According to statistical criteria, a norm may be simply defined as a 'behavior of the majority' (Perkins, 2003). The key idea behind normalization is that we need a norm reference to give significance to the raw results of the IPPJ, one which states whether the raw results vary from the average results of other persons. According to Brzeziński (2000), normalization is the procedure of creating groups of test results of persons with characteristic sets of features who are representative for the certain sample. The result of normalization is the creation of a set of norms that serves as an interpretation reference for distinct results of respondents. Norms allow a certain result to be interpreted as high, average or low and give meaning to a concrete number – the score test. Lack of a reliable and relevant reference that gives some insight into interpretation of the test score make the test and its results meaningless (Brzeziński 2000). To sum up, the psychometric norm is the standard and typical measure indicated usually by central tendency such as the mean, the median and mode.

Raw results are usually very arbitrary and depend on the construction of the test, so they need to be transformed in the standardization process. This allows for a proper interpretation of the test score, indicating whether results are high or low. It also allows for a comparison with the previous results for the same individual. The raw results of this questionnaire are represented by the ten scores and defined in relation to a standard normal distribution.

The national sample was estimated for the IPPJ-60 item version. The group of respondents included for the normalization was randomly selected, however considering following variables: gender, profile of the secondary school, region of residence.

All respondents in regard with mentioned variables was randomly selected by the SNNA (*Sistema Nacional de Nivelación y Admision*) administrative team from all secondary schools in Ecuador in regard with 3 geographical regions: Costa, Sierra and Oriente (however it was not represented well as most of the respondents: 86.1% were from the region of Sierra, and only 13.9% were for the Costa and Oriente).

The normalization sample was planned to represent well both: rural and urban area: Urban region: N-882; 37.3% and Rural region: N-1482, 62.7%.

The study that was the base for the normalization analysis was conducted in the period 13–17 of October 2014 in randomly selected secondary schools (*colegio*). The normalization sample consisted finally of the group of the 2431 students, where 1165 (49.5%) were boys and 1188 (5.5%) girls. The average age of the students included in the normalization sample was 17.68, (SD - 2.46).

The diverse profiles of the secondary education were represented by Technical Bachelor Degree (es. *Técnico Bachilerato*): N-717; 30%, General Bachelor Degree (es. *General Bachilerato*): N-1665; 68.5% and Artistic Bachelor Degree (es. *Artístico Bachilerato*): N-4; 0,2%. All students represented two regions, with the representation of the urban: N-882; 37.3% and rural region: N-1482; 62.7%.

Transformation of the raw results of the IPPJ into the standardized ten-point scale (sten scale) was the final stage of work on the questionnaire. The purpose of this procedure was to instruct occupational counselors, who on the basis of the standardized scores from the questionnaire, can then place the results of a concrete individual in relation to the representative group according to calculated group norms. The IPPJ raw results ware converted into a ten-point standardized scale (Ferguson, & Takane, 2003; Sanocki, 1976), indicating a person's estimated position with respect to the values of other people in that population (Francuz, & Mackiewicz, 2007).

The ten-point standardized scale is characterized by the following parameters: mean 5.5. SD = 2. It consists of 10 units (Table 32). The midpoint of the sten scale is the value 5.5. Each of the sten scores (score out of ten) are discriminated by half standard deviations. Table 32 shows standard scores of the stens and the percent of individuals drawn from a normal distribution with estimated sten results.

Table 32. Standard ten-point scale: percentages and sten scores

Percent	2.3%	4.4%	9.2%	15.0%	19.2%	19.2%	15.0%	9.2%	4.4%	2.3%
Sten	1	2	3	4	5	6	7	8	9	10

Each unit is equal to .5 standard deviations. In interpreting the results based on sten scores, it is assumed that a values:
- from 1 to 4 are low values,
- from 5 to 6 sten are considered average,
- from 7 and 10 sten are considered high scores.

The sten results of the IPPJ questionnaire regarding the level of intensity in a specific scale are interpreted as a preference in the direction of the indicated type of occupational inetersts. The results for each of the scales should be treated separately, but the set of 6 scales may indicate a distinct occupational interest profile of the person. Tables of standard values estimated separately for boys and girls with Norms for Holland's and Iachan's differentiation indicators and may be found in the Appendices:

6. Scales' scores calculation

How to calculate results of the study? The score for each of the IPPJ scales is calculated by arithmetically summing up the numerical results for the items constituting each scale (the key for each scale is attached in the Appendix 6.

The calculation sheet with the key (Appendix 6 and Appendix 16) is enclosed on the last page of the questionnaire and in the end serves to easily calculate the results for the 6 scales related to RIASEC interest types for the IPPJ-60 items version. All scales contain 10 items. Raw results for scales are calculated by adding up the scores obtained by the student for each item related to a certain scale. Raw results for the distinct scales must be filled in the 'row result' column next to the line entitled RS (raw score).

After the 'row results' calculation in the 6 RIASEC subscales, all results must be compared with the standard scale results for the related gender and in regard to the specific RIASEC scale from the norms table (Appendix 10–15). The score converted in this way should be related to the standardized results next to the 'Sten line'.

A graphic illustration of the results in the form of the profile is obtained by marking the appropriate bubble with the results for each of 6 scales, in correspondence to the value read from the standardized ten-point scale. The sheet lists have two forms: the table and the hexagonal profile (Appendix 16) and they indicate the standardized scores constituting each 6 RIASEC scale questionnaire. The hexagonal profile has more informative value as it was described in the theoretical introduction of the position of each of vocational types on the hexagonal model and about the consistency of the RIASEC profile.

The IPPJ results and the interpretation procedure allow additional information to be obtained to determine the degree of internal diversity and profile of occupational interests (intensity and consistency). Differentiation indicators are calculated according to the procedures specified above. These include the indicators of differentiation by Holland and Iachan. These indicators (of differentiation and intensity) are also compared with the relevant standardized norms that should be written in the relevant table on the last page of the questionnaire.

Estimating the degree of consistency in response is done with a profile check, by considering the position of the two highest scores of the hexagonal (Figure 5), which may be expressed by a two- letter code.

7. In the search of new techniques for vocational guidance practice

In addition to applying all of the assessment techniques available for more effectively assisting youth in successful construction of their career, searching for new strategies is a permanent assignment of all vocational counselors. Vocational guides should constantly look for new ways to increase youth's introspection and self-awareness by stimulating a constructive internal dialogue related to the crystallization of the vocational self.

The essence of the counseling process may be metaphorically expressed as an internal dialogue of the young person that aims to clarify their self image in their own career and the role that they should play in society. The concept of the dialogical self, proposed in the theory of Hermans and Gieser (2012), shows new perspectives for vocational guidance and the way to explore the mechanisms of affective disorders in the sphere of language, the commonly used expressions and culture. The narrative psychology approach assumes that the self is dialogical. It is inspired by the philosophy of dialogue and literature that describes the nature of the polyphonic self and may be traced to works of William James, Mikhail Bakhtin, and Martin Buber.

One of the most intriguing latest findings in psycholinguistics explains how language affects the way one thinks, feels, and perceives the world. People need to understand themselves as well the world, e.g., the reality of their career, so they develop their own implicit theories which help them to understand their vocational role, professional performance and everyday behaviors (Li-Jun, 2005).

Language is a tool of the mind that people use to categorize experience, and it organizes our own conception of the career reality and vocational self. We often experience that what we think is closely related to the language and narratives we live by (Lakoff, & Turner, 1989). Language may be seen as a mirror that reflects the thoughts of the *homo loquens* (Humboldt, 1999; Sapir, 1978, Whorf, 2002; Wittgenstein, 2000) and there is strong proof as to how language, and specifically narratives as building blocks of the self, might influence the construction of one's future career (Chiu, Krauss, & Lee, 1999; Grün, 2003).

Language is a cognitive tool that serves to categorize experiences (Turner, 1996; Whorf, 1956); hence in the mind of the user of the narratives it may evoke different mental representations of the self-image of the particular career actor.

Although empirical support for linguistic determinism, i.e. that linguistic structures determine the way we think, is limited (Glucksberg, 1988), still, language is deeply implicated in human cognition and strongly affects perception, categorization, memory, attention and problem solving processes (Hunt, & Banaji, 1991).

Narrative psychology researchers suggest that our capacity to narrate, understand, and integrate our most important *life stories* may be a key aspect in creating the image of the self (Angus, 2012; Angus, & McLeod, 2004). Many clinicians and researchers confirm the key role of self-narrative and personal stories in therapy and counseling (Baumesiter, & Newman, 1994; Berne, 2003; Bruner, 2004; Hermans, & Hermans-Jansen, 1995).

In regard to narrative psychology and the concept of the internal polyphony and dialogical self (Hermans, & Hermans-Jansen, 1995), the phenomenon of internal speech is understood as a way to connect the past experience with the ongoing present decisions of the individual. Self-narratives condition the coherence and stability over time, providing an explanation for one's different, inconsistent beliefs about the future vocational role and performance in a specific work environment (Angus, & Greenberg, 2011)

Meyer and Rowan (2012) show how the conceptual apparatus of the dialogical self describes the dynamics of psychotherapy, while Gonçalves Ribeiro (2012) shows the applicability of the dialogical self and internal narrative techniques and phases for priming new adequate paths of perception and understanding of oneself and the world in the process of vocational guidance. Valsiner (2012) describes the abstract construction process of the self (self-making) as a kind of synthesis where the self is the catalyzing space emerging in the process of constant negotiation and renegotiation of typical narratives and positions of 'I'.

An interesting mechanism in the context of the polyphonic self is the reconstruction of the most typical self-instructions that guide the way one perceives the world and oneself. Nir (2006) describes the process of internal negotiations of the dialogical self and creation of ways of resolving internal conflicts that may occur while looking for one's vocational path. And Dimaggio, Salvatore, Azzara, and Catania (2003) give examples of how to reorganize these dialogues in the process of counseling in the sphere of intra- and interpersonal dialogues.

Hermans' and Gieser's (2012) concept of the dialogical self refers to the internal speech and narratives that may arise in self-awareness, analogical to the system circulating in the community of the youth searching for their vocational self. The nature of the self is inseparably linked to the embodied experience of polyphony rooted in the social environment. This theoretical perspective tends to locate sources of possible vocational identity problems in the socio-cultural context, with an emphasis on the role of internal dialogue. An example of certain commonly used metaphoric statements related to typical strategies, the role of mistakes, as well as life strategy solutions applicable in vocational counseling is the following list of positive, constructive, and powerful proverb-like narratives that may serve in counseling practice:

- We cannot direct the wind, but we can adjust the sails.
- There is no wind that blows right for the sailor who doesn't know where the harbor is.

- Raise your sail one foot and you get ten feet of wind.
- Smooth seas do not make skillful sailors.
- Fear blows wind into your sails.
- Big ships sail on big debts.
- One should learn to sail in all winds.
- Don't sail out farther than you can row back.
- Make not your sail too big for your ballast.
- It is good rowing with the sail set.

Angus and Greenberg (2011) also view self-narrative representations as guiding future actions and note that life satisfaction often depends on how events conform to our narrative expectations. Accordingly, the verbalization and consolidation of a self through narratives becomes an important part of the constructive change process and enduring personal change.

The theoretical background of narrative psychology allows us to combine two seemingly distant fields such as vocational counseling and paremiology (the study of proverbs). Conceptual apparatus and methodology of youth' guidance based on the dialogical self concept may be considered a new promising paths for analysis of the career interests' nature and typical strategies in career navigation.

Hermans and Gieser (2012) in their work in the mainstream narrative psychology assume the system of self is constituted by the multiplicity position 'I' ('I-positions'). That narrative approach coincides with proverb thinking (Gibbs & Beitel, 2003). In this sense we may state the phenomenon of using commonly used proverbial narratives is a form of externalization of the hidden process of internal speech described by dialogical self theory and embodied in typical proverbs of, for example, individuals seeking their vocational identity. This offers a new perspective for counseling practice.

According to the narrative approach, change in self-narratives may underlie successful vocational intervention, and proverbs (as mini stories) may play a significant role to facilitate narration of specific experiences necessary to help youth in their career construction (Cunha, Spinola, & Goncalves, 2012). As such, McAdams and Janis (2004) advice that internalized self-narratives may have as much impact on guiding actions and behavior as dispositional traits and that when counselors help clients to construct new self-narrative representations, they are in fact impacting the personalities of vocational guidance clients.

We may assume that youth struggling to find their right place and path in the complex vocational reality are somehow imprisoned in their 'personal stories', struggling to define and express themselves due to their emotional and cognitive condition. In the attempt to articulate themselves, they often use the language of metaphors, images, common sayings, through which it is easier for them to capture and convey their feelings and state of mind.

Summing up, the dialogical self theory contributes to analyzing the daily discourse of youth to better understand their interests, contextualized in their education and the labor market reality and to help them to create their own successful personal story (Bruner, 2004).

Conclusions

The presented methodology of the research on occupational references of youth in Ecuador and the concrete tool *Inventario de Preferencias Profesionales de Jovenes* (IPPJ) were developed using the highest standards of psychometric tools. In addition, they obtained very satisfying validity and reliability indicators. As such, the IPPJ questionnaire may be considered to be a constructive tool in vocational guidance of youth (16–19 years old) in Ecuador. The development of such diagnostic instruments and their professional application in the practice of vocational counselors is the best indicator of expertise and professionalism, which ultimately results in high quality vocational counseling for youth in their crucial period of career decision-making and school-to work transition process.

According to the legal regulations in Ecuador, educational institutions, especially secondary schools are obliged to provide youth with valid and appropriate vocational guidance services to prepare them to perform effectively in the workplace. Psychologists and vocational guides employed in schools are responsible for this task. One of the conditions for fulfilling the mission of youth guidance is the continuous development of professional skills, knowledge, and psychometric methods to increase the reliability and quality of vocational guidance. The tool described in this book aspires to impact the occupational choices and improve the quality of life and well being (*Sumak Kawsay*) of future workers in Ecuador.

In the fast-paced present day reality with its major shifts in high technology, it will be necessary to update existing diagnostic tools such as IPPJ and develop new ones. Additionally, the successful IPPJ construction project opens new research perspectives to better understand mechanisms that guide occupational choices of youth. One of these upcoming projects is establishing a longitudinal study to review the prognostic power of the IPPJ, based on the group of tested individuals who will likely settle into a career path, performing a concrete job. Another research perspective is including additional variables that might highlight new factors of occupational preferences, such as the culture of the diverse Ecuadorian society, parents' occupation and socioeconomic situation of youth.

Bibliography

Achtnich, M. (1979). *Der Berufsbilder-Test. Projektives Verfahren zur Abklarung der Berufsneigung.* Bern, Stuttgart, Wien: Verlan Hans Huber.

Achtnich, M. (1987). *Der Berufsbildertest. Seine Anwendung in der Berufs- und Laufbahnberatung – eine Einführung.* Bern: Hans Huber

Aiken, J., & Johnston, J.A. (1973). Promoting career information seeking behaviors in college students. *Journal of Vocational Behavior. 3.* 81–87.

A Memorandum on Lifelong Learning (2000). Brussels: Commission of the European Communities.

Anastasi, A., & Urbina, S. (1999). *Testy Psychologiczne* [Psychological testing]. Warszawa: Pracownia Testów Psychologicznych PTS.

Angus, L. (2012). An integrative understanding of narrative and emotion processes in Emotion-focused therapy of depression: Implications for theory, research and practice. *Psychotherapy Research, 22,* 367–380.

Angus, L., & Greenberg, L. (2011). *Working with narrative in emotion-focused therapy: Changing stories, healing lives.* Washington, DC: American Psychological Association Press.

Angus, L., & J. McLeod (eds.) (2004). *The handbook of narrative and psychotherapy: Practice, theory and research* (pp. 159–174). Thousand Oaks, CA: Sage Press.

Athanasou, J.A., & Van Esbroeck, R. (eds.). (2008). *International Handbook of Career Guidance.* Dordrecht: Springer.

Bajcar, B., & Gąsiorowska, A. (2006). Zmiana paradygmatu diagnozy zainteresowań w doradztwie zawodowym [Change the paradigm of interest diagnosis in career counseling]. In: *Testy w poradnictwie zawodowym. Zeszyty Informacyjno-Metodyczne Doradcy Zawodowego, 37,* 77–98. Warszawa: Ministerstwo Pracy i Polityki Społecznej.

Ballantine, M. (1986). Computer-assisted careers guidance systems as decision support systems. *British Journal of Guidance and Counselling, 14,* 21–32.

Bambra, C., & Eikemo, T. (2009). Welfare state regimes, unemployment and health: a comparative study of the relationship between unemployment and self-reported health in 23 European countries. *Journal of Epidemiology &Community Health, 63,* 92–98.

Bandura, A. (2001). Social cognitive theory: An agentic perspective. *Annual review of psychology, 52,* 1–26.

Bandura, A., Barbaranelli, C., Caprara, G.V., & Pastorelli, C. (2001). Self-efficacy beliefs as shapers of children's aspirations and career trajectories. *Child Development, 72,* 187–206.

Bańka, A. (1995). *Zawodoznawstwo, doradztwo zawodowe i pośrednictwo pracy* [Knowledge of professions, vocational guidance, and Job placement]. Poznań: Print-B.

Barak, A., & Rabi, B. (1981). Predicting persistent. Stability and achievement in college by major choice consistency: A test of Holland's consistency hypothesis. *Journal of Vocational Behavior, 20,* 235–243.

Barrick, M.R., Mount, M.K., & Gupta, R. (2003). Meta analysis of the relationship between the five-factor model of personality and Holland's occupational types. *Personel Psychology, 56,* 45–74.

Bastidas, P. (2003). *Inventario Tipologico Temperamental.* Quito: UCE.

Baumeister, R.F., & Newman, L.S. (1994). How stories make sense of personal experiences: Motives that shape autobiographical narratives. *Personality and Social Psychology Bulletin, 20,* 676–690.

Beauvale, A., Noworol, Cz., & Łącała, Z. (1998). *Bateria Testów Uzdolnień Ogólnych* [General Aptitude Test Battery] Warszawa: MPiPS. KUP.

Bentler, P.M., & Bonett, D.G. (1980). Significance tests and goodness of fit in the analysis of covariance structures. *Psychological Bulletin,* 88, 588–606. doi:1.1037/0033-2909.88.3.588.

Berne, E. (2003). *W co grają ludzie* [Games people play], Warszawa: Wydawnictwo Naukowe PWN.

Betsworth, D. G., Bouchard, T.J., Jr., Cooper, C.R., Grotevant, H.D., Hansen, J.I.C., & Scarr, S. (1994). Genetic and environmental influences on vocational interests assessed using adoptive and biological families and twins reared apart and together. *Journal of Vocational Behavior, 44,* 263–278.

Bimrose, J., Barnes, S.A., & Hughes, D. (2008). *Adult Career Progression and Advancement: a Five Year Study of the Effectiveness of Guidance.* Coventry: Warwick Institute for Employment Research and the Department for Innovation. Universities and Skills.

Borman, W.C., Hanson, M.A., & Hedge, J.W. (1997). Personnel selection. *Annual Review of Psychology, 48,* 299–337.

Brown, D. (2002). *Career Choice and Development.* San Francisco: Jossey-Bass.

Brown, D., & Brooks, L. (1984). Introduction to career development: origins. evolution. and current approaches. In: D. Brown. L. Brooks (eds.). *Career choice and development* (pp. 1–7). San Francisco. Washington. London: Jossey-Bass Publishers.

Brown, T.A. (2006). *Confirmatory Factor Analysis for Applied Research.* New York–London: The Guilford Press.

Bruner, J. (2004). The narrative creation of self. In: L. Angus & J. McLeod (eds.), *The handbook of narrative and psychotherapy: Practice, theory and research* (pp. 3–14). Thousand Oaks, CA: Sage Press.

Brzezińska, A. (2000). *Społeczna psychologia rozwoju* [Social psychology of development]. Warszawa: Wydawnictwo Naukowe Scholar.

Brzeziński, J. (2000). *Badania eksperymentalne w psychologii i pedagogice* [Experimental research i psychology and pedagogy]. Warszawa: Scholar.

Brzeziński, J. (2006). *Metodologia badań psychologicznych* [Psychological research methodology] (5th ed.). Warszawa: Wydawnictwo Naukowe PWN.

Brzozowski, P. (2007). *Wzorcowa hierarchia wartości* [Model hierarchy of values]. Lublin: Wydawnictwo Uniwersytetu Marii Curie-Skłodowskiej.

Bysshe, S., Hughes D., & Bowes L. (2002). *The Economic Benefits of Guidance: a Review of Current Evidence.* CeGS Occ.

Campbell, D.P. (1971). *Handbook for the SVIB.* Stanford, Calif.: Stanford University Press.

Cattell, R.B. (1957). *Personality and motivation structure and measurement.* New York: World Book.

Cattell, R.B. (1971). *Abilities: Their structure, growth and action.* Boston, USA: Houghton Mifflin.

Cattell, R.B. (1978). *The scientific use of factor analysis.* New York: Plenum.

Chauvin, I., Müler, M.J., Godfrey, E.L., & Thomas, D. (2010). Relationship between Holland's Vocational Typology and Myers-Briggs' Types: Implications for Career Counselors. *Psychology Journal, 7,* 61–66.

Chiu, C., Krauss, R.M., & Lee, S.L. (1999). Communication and social cognition: A post-Whorfian approach. In: T. Sugiman, M. Karasawa, J.H. Liu, & Ward, C. (eds.), *Progress in Asian social psychology* (Vol. II, pp. 127–143). Hong Kong: Kyoyook-kwahak-sa.

Comrey, A.L., & Lee H.B. (1992). *A first course in factor analysis* (2nd ed.). Hillsdale. NJ: Erlbaum.

Costa, P.T, McCrae, R.R. (1992). The five-factor model of personality and its relevance to personality disorders. *Journal of Personality Disorders, 6,* 343–359.

Costa, P.T., McCrae, R.R., & Holland, J.L. (1984). Personality and vocational interests in an adult sample. *Journal of Applied Psychology, 69,* 390–400.

Crocker, L., & Algina, J. (1986). *Introduction to classical and modern test theory.* New York: Holt, Rinehart and Winston.

Cronbach, L.J. (1951). Coefficient alpha and the internal structure of tests. *Psychometrika, 16,* 297–334.

Cunha, C.A.C., Joana Spinola, J., & Goncalves, M.M. (2012). The Emergence of Innovative Moments in Narrative Therapy for expression: Exploring Therapist and Client Contributions, *Research in Psychotherapy: Psychopathology, Process and Outcome, 15,* 62–74.

Davis, F.P. (1964). *Educational measurement and their interpretation.* Belmont, Calif.: Wadsworth.

Demerouti, E., Bakker. A.B., Nachreiner, F., & Schaufeli. W.B. (2001). The Job Demands-Resources model of burnout. *Journal of Applied Psychology, 86,* 499–512.

Dimaggio, G., Salvatore, G., Azzara, C., & Catania, D. (2003). Rewriting self-narratives: The therapeutic process. *Journal of Constructivist Psychology, 16,* 155–181.

Drabik-Podgórna, V., & Podgórny, M. (2006). Problèmes liés à l'orientation des jeunes dans la région *Polonaise de Wałbrzych, Orientation Scolaire et Professionnelle, 35,* 205–224.

Eggerth, D.E. (2008). From Theory of Work Adjustment to Person-Environment Correspondence Counseling: Vocational Psychology as Positive Psychology. *Journal of Career Assessment, 16,* 60–74.

Eliasz, A. (1981). *Temperament jako system regulacji stymulacji* [Temperament as a system of regulation of stimulation]. Warszawa: PWN.

Erwin, T.D. (1982). The construct validity of Holland's construct of consistency. *Journal of Vocational Behavior, 20,* 180–192.

Eysenck, H.J., & Eysenck, S.B.G. (1976). *Psychoticism as a Dimension of Personality.* London: Hodder & Stoughton.

Fairholm, M.R. (2013). *Putting your values to work: becoming the leader others want to follow.* Praeger: Santa Barbara.

Ferguson, G.A., & Takane. Y. (1999). *Analiza statystyczna w psychologii i pedagogice* [Statistical analysis in psychology and pedagogy]. Warszawa: Wydawnictwo Naukowe PWN.

Field, A. (2005). *Discovering statistics using SPSS.* London: Sage Publications.

Fogliatto, H., Pérez, E., Olaz, F., & Parodi, L. (2003). Cuestionario de Intereses Profesionales Revisado. (CIP-R). *Análisis de sus Propiedades Psicométricas. Evaluar, 3,* 61–78.

Fouad, N.L., & Dancer, L.S. (1992). Cross-cultural structure of interests: Mexico and the United States. *Journal of Vocational Behavior, 40,* 129–143.

Francuz, P., & Mackiewicz, R. (2007). *Liczby nie wiedzą, skąd pochodzą. Przewodnik po metodologii i statystyce nie tylko dla psychologów* [Numbers do not know where they come from. Guide to methodology and statistics not only for psychologists], Lublin: Wydawnictwo KUL.

Fuller, B.E., Holland, J.L., & Johnston, J.A. (1999). The relation of profile elevation in the self-directed search to personality variables. *Journal of Career Assessment, 7,* 111–123.

Gardner, H. (2002). *Inteligencje wielorakie. Teoria w praktyce* [Multiple Intelligences. Theory in practice]. Poznań: Media Rodzina.

Gardner, H., Kornhaber M.L., & Wake. W.K. (2001). *Inteligencja. Wielorakie perspektywy* [Intelligence. Multiple perspectives]. Warszawa: WSiP.

Gati, I., & Asher, I. (2001). The PIC model for career decision making: Prescreening, indepth exploration, and choice. In: F.T. Leong & A. Barak (eds.). *Contemporary models in vocational psychology* (pp. 7–54). Mahwah. NJ: Lawrence Erlbaum Associates.

Gati, I., Fishman-Nadav, Y., & Shiloh, S. (2006). The relations between preferences for using abilities. self-estimated abilities. and measured abilities among career counseling clients. *Journal of Vocational Bahavior, 68,* 24–38.

Gati, I., Kleiman, T., Saka, N., & Zakai. A. (2003). Perceived benefits of using an Internetbased interactive career planning system. *Journal of Vocational Behavior, 62,* 272–286.

Gati, I., Osipow, S.H., & Givon. M. (1995). Gender differences in career decision making: The content and structure of preferences. *Journal of Counseling Psychology, 42,* 204–216.

Gati, I., & Ram, G. (2000). Counselors' judgments of the quality of the prescreening stage of the career decision-making process. *Journal of Counseling Psychology, 47,* 414–428.

Gati, I., Saka, N., & Krausz. M. (2001). 'Should I Use a Computer-Assisted Career Guidance System?' It Depends on Where Your Career Decision-Making Difficulties Lie. *British Journal of Guidance & Counselling, 29,* 301–321.

Geist, H. (1970). *The Geist Picture Interest Inventory.* California, USA: M.M.

Gibbs, R.W., & Beitel, D. (2003). What Proverb Understanding Reveals About How People Think. In: Wolfgang Mieder (2003), *Comprehension, Communication, A Decade of North American Proverb Studies (1990–2000)*. Schneider Verlag: Hohengehren.

Ginzberg, B. (1984). Career development. In: D. Brown and L. Brooks (eds.) *Career choice and development: Applying contemporary theories to practice*. San Francisco. OA: Jossey-Bass.

Glucksberg, S. (1988). Language and thought. In: R.S. Sternberg & E.E. Smith (eds.), *The psychology of human thought* (pp. 214–241). New York: Cambridge University Press.

Gonçalves, M.M., & Ribeiro, A. (2012). Narrative processes of innovation and stability within the dialogical self. In: H.J.M. Hermans & T. Gieser (eds.), *Handbook of Dialogical Self Theory*. Cambridge: Cambridge University Press.

Gordon V.N. (1998). Career Decidedness Types: A Literature Review. *The Career Development Quarterly, 46,* 386–403.

Gottfredson, G.D., & Holland, J.L. (1996). *Dictionary of Holland occupational codes* (3rd ed.). Odessa. FL: Psychological Assessment Resources.

Gottfredson, G.D., & Lipstein, D.J. (1975). Using personal characteristics to predict parolee and probationer employment stability. *Journal of Applied Psychology, 60,* 644–648.

Gottfredson, L.S., & Richards, J.M. (1999). The Meaning and Measurement of Environments in Holland's Theory. *Journal of Vocational Behavior, 55,* 57–73.

Grieve, R., & Mahar, D. (2013). Can social intelligence be measured? Psychometric properties of the Tromsø Social Intelligence Scale – English Version. *The Irish Journal of Psychology, 34,* 1–12.

Grün, A. (2003). *Autosugestia – jak myśleć pozytywnie* [Autosuggestion – how to think positively]. Katowice: WAM.

Guadagnoli, E., & Velicer, W. (1988). Relation of sample size to the stability of component patterns. *Psychological Bulletin, 103,* 265–272.

Guichard, J., & Huteau, M. (2005). *Psychologia orientacji i poradnictwa zawodowego* [Psychology of vocational guidance and career counselling]. Kraków: Oficyna Wydawnicza „Impuls".

Guiford, J.P. (2005). Rzetelność i trafność pomiarów [Reliability and validity]. In: J. Brzeziński (eds.) *Trafność i rzetelność testów psychologicznych.* Gdańsk: Gdańskie Wydawnictwo Psychologiczne.

Gurycka, A. (1978). *Rozwój i kształtowanie zainteresowań* [Development and shaping of interests]. Warszawa: Wydawnictwa Szkolne i Pedagogiczne.

Harrington, T.F., Feller, R., & O'Shea, A.J., (1993). Four methods to determine RIASEC codes for college majors and a comparison of hit rates. *The Career Development Quarterly, 41,* 383–392.

Harrington, T.F., & Long, J. (2013). The History of Interest Inventories and Career Assessments in Career Counseling. *The Career Development Quarterly, 61,* 83–93.

Hermans, H.J., & Gieser, T. (2012). (ed.). *Handbook of Dialogical Self Theory*. New York: Cambridge University Press.

Hermans, J.M., & Hermans-Jansen, E. (1995). *Self-narratives: The construction of meaning in psychotherapy*. New York: Guilford Press.

Herr, E.L., & Cramer, S.H. (1996). *Career guidance and counseling through the lifespan: Systematic approaches*. New York: Harper Collins.

Hirschi, A., & Leg, D. (2007). Holland's secondary constructs of vocational interests and career choice readiness of secondary students. *Journal of Individual Differences, 28,* 205– 218.

Ho, R. (2006). *Handbook of univariate and multivariate data analysis and interpretation with SPSS*. London–New York: Boca Raton. Taylor and Francis Group.

Holland, J.L. (1959). A theory of vocational choice. *Journal of Counseling Psychology, 6,* 35–45.

Holland, J.L. (1975). *Manual for the Vocational Preference Inventory*. Palo Alto. CA: Consulting Psychologists Press.

Holland, J.L. (1985). *Manual for the Vocational Preference Inventory*. Odessa. FL: Psychological Assessment Resources.

Holland, J.L. (1992). *Vocational exploration and insight kit*. Odessa. FL: Psychological Assessment Resources.

Holland, J.L. (1994). *The Self-Directed Search* (4th ed.). Odessa. FL: Psychological Assessment Resources.

Holland, J.L. (1997). *Making vocational choices: A theory of vocational personalities and work environments* (3rd ed.). Odessa FL: Psychological Assessment Resources.

Holland, J.L., & Associates. (1980). *Counselor's guide to the Vocational Exploration and Insight Kit (VEIK)*. Palo Alto. CA: Consulting Psychologists Press.

Holland. J.L., Gottfredson. D.C., & Power. P.G. (1980). Some diagnostic scales for research in decision making and personality: Identity, information, and barriers. *Journal of Personality and Social Psychology, 39*, 191–220.

Holland. J.L., & Gottfredson. G.D., Nafziger D.H. (1975). Testing the validity of some theoretical signs of vocational decision-making ability. *Journal of Counseling Psychology, 22*, 411–422.

Holland, J.L., Powell, A., & Fritzsche, B. (1994). *The Self-directed Search: Professional User's Guide*. Odessa, FL: Psychological Assessment Resources.

Holland. J.L., & Rayman. J.R. (1986). The Self-Directed Search. In: W.B. Walsh & S.H. Osipow (eds.). *Advances in vocational psychology: The assessment of interests* (pp. 55–82). Hillsdale. NJ: Erlbaum.

Holland. J.L., Sorensen. A.B., Clark J.P., Nafziger D.H. & Blum. Z.D. (1973). Applying an occupational classification to a representative sample of work histories. *Journal of Applied Psychology, 58*, 34–41.

Holland. J.L., Whitney. D.R., Cole. N.S., & Richards. J.M. (1969). *An empirical occupational classification derived from a theory of personality and intended for practice and research* (ACT Research Report No. 29). Iowa City. IA: American College Testing Program.

Holland. J.L., Whitney. D.R., Cole. N.S., & Richards. J.M. Jr. (1973). *An empirical occupational classification derived from a theory of personality and intended for practice and research* (ACT Research Report No. 29). Iowa City. IA: American College Testing.

Hornowska, E. (2007). *Testy psychologiczne. Teoria i praktyka* [Psychological testig. Theory and practice]. Warszawa: Wydawnictwo Naukowe "Scholar".

Hornowski, B. (1978). *Rozwój inteligencji i uzdolnień specjalnych* [Development of intelligence and special apptitudes]. Warszawa: WSiP.

Hoyle, R.H. (2011). *Structural equation modeling for social and personality.* Thousand Oaks, CA: Sage.

Hu, L.T., & Bentler, P.M. (1995). Evaluating model fit. In: R.H. Hoyle (ed.), *Structural equation modeling: Concepts, issues and applications* (pp. 76–99). Thousand Oaks, CA: Sage.

Hu, L., & Bentler, P.M. (1998). Fit indices in covariance structure modeling: Sensitivity to underparameterized model misspecification. *Psychological Methods, 3*, 424–453.

Hu, L., & Bentler, P.M. (1999). Cutoff criteria for fit indexes in covariance structure analysis: Conventional criteria versus new alternatives. *Structural Equation Modeling, 6*, 1–55, doi: 1.1080/10705519909540118.

Humboldt, W. (1999). Humboldt: On Language: On the Diversity of Human Language Construction and its Influence on the Mental Development of the Human Species. In: M. Losonsky (ed.), *Cambridge Texts in the History of Philosophy*, (transl. P. Heath), New York: Cambridge University Press.

Hunt, E., & Banaji, M.R. (1991). The Whorfian hypothesis: A cognitive psychology perspective. *Psychological Review, 98*, 377–389.

Hutcheson, G., & Sofroniou, N. (1999). *Multivariate social scientist.* London: Sage.

Iachan, R. (1984). A measure of agreement for use with the Holland classification system. *Journal of Vocational Behavior, 24*, 133–141.

INEC (Instituto Nacional De Estadística y Censos) (2010a). *National Population Census*, 201. In Ministerio de Inclusión Económica y Social, Dirección Nacional de la Juventud, Secretaría Nacional del Migrante, Organización Iberoamericana de Juventud, Programa Conjunto "Juventud, Empleo y Migración."

INEC (Instituto Nacional De Estadística y Censos). (2010b), Condiciones de Vida Según Nivel de Preparación Académica, 201. In Ministerio de Inclusión Económica y Social, Dirección Nacional de la Juventud, Secretaría Nacional del Migrante, Organización Iberoamericana de Juventud, Programa Conjunto "Juventud, Empleo y Migración."

Johnson, J. (2013). Selfless Service, Part II: Different Types of Seva. *Psychology Today.* June 19.

Judge, T.A., Klinger R.L., & Simon L.S. (2010). Time Is on My Side: Time. General Mental Ability. Human Capital. and Extrinsic Career Success. *Journal of Applied Psychology, 95*, 92–107.

Jung, C.J. (1921). *Psychologische Typen.* Rascher Verlag: Zurich.

Kaiser, H.F. (1974). An index of factorial simplicity. *Psychometrica, 39,* 401–415.

Kalwij, A.F., & Vermeulen, F. (2008). Health and Labour Force Participation of Older People in Europe: What Do Objective Health Indicators Add to the Analysis?, *Health Economics, 17,* 619–638.

Karwowska-Szulkin, R., & Strelau, J. (1990). Reactivity and the stimulative value of managerial styles. *Polish Psychological Bulletin, 21,* 49–6.

Kass, R.A., & Tinsley, H.E.A. (1979). Factor analysis. *Journal of Leisure Research, 11,* 120–138.

Kazdin, A.E. (ed.). (2000). *Encyclopedia of Psychology.* Washington, DC: American Psychological Association.

Keirsey, D., & Bates, M. (1984). *Please Understand Me: Character & Temperament Types.* Prometheus Nemesis Book Company: Del Mar.

Kleiman, T., & Gati, I. (2004) Challenges of Internet-Based Assessment: Measuring Career Decision--Making Difficulties. *Measurement and Evaluation in Counseling and Development, 37,* 41–56.

Kline, R.B. (2005). *Principles and practice of structural equation modeling.* New York: Guilford Press.

Kreft, W., Sołtysińska, G., Łukaszewicz, A., & Dankowska, R. (2000). Podręczniki oceny zawodów z punktu widzenia różnych niepełnosprawności [Handbooks for assessing professions from the point of view of different disabilities]. *Zeszyty informacyjno-metodyczne doradcy zawodowego.* Warszawa: Krajowy Urząd Pracy.

Krumboltz, J.D. (1979). A social learning theory of career decision making. In: Mitchell A.M., Jones G.B., Krumboltz J.D. (ed.). *Social learning and career decision making* (pp. 19– 49). Cranston: The Caroll Press.

Łącała, Z., Noworol C., & Beauvale A. (1998). *Zestaw do Samobadania ZdS – Wersja S* [The Self-Directed Search – S version]. Warszawa: Ministerstwo Pracy i Polityki Socjalnej. Krajowy Urząd Pracy.

Lakoff, G., & Turner, M. (1989). *More than Cool Reason: A Field Guide to Poetic Metaphor.* Chicago: University of Chicago Press.

Laton, J.R. (1989). Consistency of Holland code and its relation to persistence in college major. *Journal of Vocational Behavior, 34,* 253–265.

Lelińska, K. (2006). *Zawodoznawstwo w planowaniu kariery* [Knowledge abouy vocations incareer planning]. Warszawa: OHP.

Lennick, D., & Kiel, F. (2007). *Inteligencja moralna* [Moral intelligence]. Wrocław: Purana.

Lent, R.W., & Brown, S.D. (eds.), (2005). *Career development and counseling: Putting theory and research to work.* Hoboken, NJ, US: John Wiley & Sons Inc.

Lent, R.W., Brown, S.D. & Hacket, G. (1994). Toward a unifying social cognitive theory of career and academic interests, choice, and performance. *Journal of Vocational Behavior, 45,* 79–122.

Leong, F.T.L. (1991). Career development attributes and occupational values of Asian American and White American College Students. *Career Development Quarterly, 39,* 221–223.

Leung, S.A., Conoley, C.W., Scheel, M.J., & Sonnenberg, R.T. (1992). An examination of relation between vocational identity, consistency, and differentiation. *Journal of Vocational Behavior, 4,* 95–107.

Lifelong Guidance Policies: Work in Progress. A report on the work of the European Lifelong Guidance Policy Network 2008–10 (2010). Jyvaskyla. Finland: University of Jyvaskyla. European Lifelong Guidance Policy Network (ELGPN) Finnish Institute for Educational Research (FIER).

Li-Jun, J. (2005). Culture and lay theory of change, In: R.M. Sorrentino, D. Cohen (ed.). *Culture and Social Behaviour. The Ontario Symposium, 10,* 117-136, Mahwah, New Jersey: Lawrence Erlbaum Associates.

López, M.V. (2000). *Inventario de Intereses y Preferencias Profesionales.* Madrid, Espala: TEA Ediciones.

Lopez-Acevedo, G. (2002). *School Attendance and Child Labor in Ecuador.* World Bank – Poverty and Economic Management Unit. World Bank Policy Research Working Paper No. 2939.

Lowman, R.L., & Carson, A.D. (2003). *Handbook of Psychology,* Medford, MA: Wiley Online Library.

MacCallum, R.C., Brown, M., & Sugawara, H.M. (1996). Power analysis and determinantion of sample size for covariance structure modeling. *Psychological Methods, 1,* 130–149.

MacCallum, R.C., Widaman, K.F., Zhang, S., & Hong, S. (1999). Sample size in factor analysis. *Psychological Methods, 4*, 84–89.

Mann, L., Harmoni, R., Power, C., Beswick, G., & Ormond, C. (1988). Effectiveness of the GOFER course in decision making for high school students. *Journal of Behavioral Decision Making, 1*, 159–168.

Matczak, A. (1991). Próba kwestionariuszowego pomiaru zainteresowań młodzieży [Attempt of questionnaire measurement of youth interest]. *Psychologia Wychowawcza, 34*, 151–163.

Mayer, J.I., & Salovey, P. (1997). What is emotional intelligence? In: P. Salovey & I. Sluyter (eds.). *Emotional development and emotional intelligence. Implications for educators.* New York: State University, Basic Books.

McAdams, D.P., & Janis, L. (2004). *The handbook of narrative and psychotherapy: Practice, theory, and research.* Thousand Oaks, CA, US: Sage Publications.

Meir, E.I. (1989). Integrative elaboration of the congruence theory. *Journal of Vocational Behavior, 35*, 219–223.

Meyer, H.D. & Rowan, B. (2012). *New Institutionalism in Education*, New York: State University of New York Press.

Michell, J. (1999). *Measurement in Psychology.* Cambridge: Cambridge University Press.

Ministerio Coordinador de Patrimonio Natural y Cultural [National Institute of Cultural Heritage] (2008). *Informe de Labores 2007–2008.* Quito: SobocGrafic.

Ministerio de Cultura del Ecuador (2008), Instituto Nacional de Patrimonio Cultural y Ministerio Coordinador de Patrimonio Natural y Cultural. *Ecuador un maravilloso cofre de tesoros.* Quito: Manthra Editores.

Misamichi, S. (1998). *Values and attitudes across nations and time.* Brill: Leiden.

Mitchell, L.K., & Krumboltz, J.D. (1996). Krumboltz's learning theory of career choice and counseling. In: D. Brown & L. Brooks (eds.), *Career choice and development* (3rd ed.), (pp. 233–280). San Francisco: Jossey-Bass.

Nauta, M.M. (2010). The development, evolution, and status of Holland's theory of vocational personalities: Reflections and future directions for counseling psychology. *Journal of Counseling Psychology, 57*, 11–22.

Nauta, M.M., & Kahn, J.H. (2007). Identity status, consistency and differentiation of interests, and career decision self-efficacy. *Journal of Career Assessment, 15*, 55–65.

Nęcka, E. (2003). *Inteligencja. Geneza, struktura, funkcje* [Intelligence. Genesis, structure and functions]. Gdańsk: Gdańskie Wydawnictwo Psychologiczne.

Nęcka, E. (2004). Inteligencja. In: J. Strelau (ed.). *Psychologia. Podręcznik akademicki* [Psychology. Academic manual] (vol. 1. pp. 721–760). Gdańsk: Gdańskie Wydawnictwo Psychologiczne.

Nevill, D.D., & Schlecher, D.T. (1988). The relationship of self-efficacy and assertiveness to willingness to engage in traditional/ nontraditional career activities. *Psychology of Women Quarterly, 12*, 91–98.

Nevill, D.D., & Super, D.E. (1986). *The values scate manual.* Palo Alto, CA: Consulting Psychologists Press.

Nir, D. (2011). Voicing inner conflict: From a dialogical to a negotiational self. In: H. Hermans & T. Gieser (eds.), *Handbook of Dialogical Self Theory* (pp. 284–300). Cambridge: Cambridge University Press.

Normativa departamento de consejeria estudiantil en establecimientos. (2014). Acuerdo Ministerial 69. Registro Oficial Suplemento 143 de 2.06.2014. No. 0069-14. Augusto X. Espinosa A. Ministro de Educacion.

Nowakowska, M. (1975). *Psychologia ilościowa z elementami naukometrii* [Quantitative psychology with elements of science] Warszawa: Państwowe Wydawnictwo Naukowe.

Nunnally, J.C. (1978). *Psychometric theory.* New York: McGraw-Hill.

O'Neil, J., & Magoon, T.M. (1977). The predictability of Holland's investigative personality types and consistency levels using the Self-Directed Search. *Journal of Vocational Behavior, 10*, 39–46.

Oakland, T., Stafford, M., Horton, C., & Glutting, J. (2001). Temperament and vocational preferences: Age, gender and racial-ethnic comparisons using the Student Styles Questionnaire. *Journal of Career Assessment, 9*, 297–314.

OIT (eng. ILO), (2011). Perfiles del Empleo y Trabajo Decente en América Latina y el Caribe. In Jóvenes Ecuatorianos en Cifras.

Oleszkiewicz-Zsurzs, Z. (1986). Zapotrzebowanie na stymulację a preferencje do wyboru zawodu [Demand for stimulation and preferences to choose a profession]. *Przegląd Psychologiczny, 29*, 509–526.

Osipow, S.H., & Fitzgerald, L.F. (1996). *Theories of Career Development.* Needham Heights. Massachusetts: Allyn & Bacon.

Ott-Holland, C.J., Huang, J.L., Ryan, A.M., Elizondo, F. & Wadlington, P.L. (2013). Culture and vocational interests: The moderating role of collectivism and gender egalitarianism. *Journal of Counseling Psychology, 60*, 569–581.

Overton, W.F. (2010). Life-span development: Concepts and issues. In: W.F. Overton & R. M. Lerner (eds.), *The handbook of life-span development*, vol. 1: *Cognition, biology, and methods* (pp. 1–29). Hoboken, NJ: John Wiley & Sons, Inc.

Paessler, K. (2015). Sex differences in variability in vocational interests: Evidence from two large samples. *European Journal of Personality, 29*, 568–578.

Paszkowska-Rogacz, A. (ed.) (2010). *Parents as counsellors of their children.* Saarbrüucken: Lambert Academic Publishing.

Paszkowska-Rogacz, A. (2011). *Podręcznik. Młodzieżowy Kwestionariusz Zainteresowań Młodzieży MŁOKOZZ* [Manual. Preference Questionnaire for Youth]. Kraków: Drukarnia Pasaż Sp. z o.o.

Perkins, H.W. (2003). *The Social Norms Approach to Preventing School and College Age Substance Abuse: A Handbook for Educators, Counselors, and Clinicians.* San Francisco: Jossey-Bass.

Ponce, J. (2004). *Etnicidad y educación en el Ecuador [Ethnicity and education in Ecuador].* Paper given at the 8th Ecuadorian Congress of Sociology and Latin American Meeting of Social Sciences, Quito, July 2004, FLACSO-Ecuador, Quito, July 2004. Fronesis Institute website.

Prediger, D.J. (1999). Basic structure of work-relevant abilities. *Journal of Counseling Psychology, 46*, 173–184.

Prediger, D.J. (2004). Career planning validity of self-estimates and test estimates of work relevant abilities. *Career Development Quarterly, 52*, 202–211.

Prediger, D.J. Swaney, K., & Mau, K.W. (1993). The world-of-work map. *Journal of Counseling & Development, 71*, 422–428.

Prediger, D.J., & Vansickle T.R. (1992). Locating occupations on Holland's hexagon: beyond RIASEC. *Journal of Vocational Behaviour, 4*, 111–128.

Rosen, D., Holmberg, K., & Holland, J.L. (1989). *The college majors finder.* Odessa. FL: Psychological Assessment Resources. Inc.

Rossier, J. (2015). Personality assessment and career interventions. In: P.J. Hartung, M.L. Savickas, W.B. Walsh, (eds.) *APA Handbook of Career Intervention*, vol. 1: *Foundations.* American Psychological Association.

Rounds, J., & Tracey, T.J.G. (1996). Cross-cultural structural equivalence of RIASEC models and measures. *Journal of Counseling Psychology, 43*, 310–329.

Sanocki, W. (1976). *Kwestionariusze osobowości w psychologii* [Personality questionnaires in psychology]. Warszawa: PWN.

Sapir, E. (1978). *Kultura, język, osobowość* [Culture, language, personality]. Warszawa: PIW.

Savickas, M.L. (2005). The theory and practice of career construction. In: R.W. Lent & S.D. Brown (eds.). *Career development and counseling: Putting theory and research to work* (pp. 42–70). Hoboken, New York: Wiley.

Savickas, M.L. (2012). Constructing Careers: Actors, Agents, and Authors. *The Counseling Psychologist*, XX(X), 1–15, DOI: 1.1177/0011000012468339.

Savickas, M.L., & Lent, R. (1994). *Convergence in Career Development Theories.* Palo Alto. California: Consulting Psychologists Press.

Schein, E.H., (2006). *Career anchors.* San Francisco: Pfeiffer, Imprint of Wiley.

Schermer, A.J., Petrides, K.V., & Vernon, P.A. (2015). On the Genetic and Environmental Correlations between Trait Emotional Intelligence and Vocational Interest Factors. *Twin Research and Human Genetics, 18*, 134–137.

Schiefele, U., Krapp, A., Winteler, A. (1992). Interests as a predictor of academic achievement: A meta analysis of research. In: K.A. Renninger. S. Hidi. A. Krapp (eds.). *The role of interests in learning and development* (pp. 183–212). Hillsdale. NJ: Erlbaum.

Schraw, G., & Lehman, S. (2001). Situational interests: A review of the literature and directions for future research. *Educational Psychology Review, 134*, 23–52.

Schwartz, S.H., & Bilsky, W. (1990). Toward a theory of the universal content and structure of values: Extensions and cross cultural replications. *Journal of Personality and Social Psychology, 58*, 878–891.

Shin, Y., & Kelly, K.R. (2013), Cross-Cultural Comparison of the Effects of Optimism, Intrinsic Motivation, and Family Relations on Vocational Identity. *The Career Development Quarterly, 61*, 141–160.

Slaney, R.B. (1980). Expressed Vocational Choice and Vocational Indecision. *Journal of Counseling Psychology, 27*, 122–129.

Soulière, M.D., MacPhee, M.C., & Flynn, R.J. (1991). Concurrent and predictive validity of Prediger's two work-task preference dimensions. *Journal of Vocational Behavior, 39*, 226–224.

Spearman, C. (1904). "General intelligence" objectively determined and measured. *American Journal of Psychology, 15*, 201–293.

Standardy dla testów stosowanych w psychologii i pedagogice [Standards for tests used in psychology and pedagogy] (2006), Gdańsk: Gdańskie Wydawnictwo Psychologiczne.

Stein, M.A. (2010). Labor Markets, Rationality, and Workers with Disabilities. *Berkeley Journal of Employment and Labor Law, 21*, 314–334.

Sternberg, R.J. (2001). *Psychologia poznawcza* [Cognitive psychology]. Warszawa: WSiP.

Sternberg, R.J., & Salter, W. (1982). *Handbook of human intelligence.* Cambridge, UK: Cambridge University Press.

Stevens, J.P. (1992). *Applied multivariate statistics for the social sciences* (2nd ed.). Hillsdale. NJ: Erlbaum.

Strauser, D.R., Lustig, D.C., & Ciftci, A. (2008). Psychological well-being: Its relation to work personality, vocational identity, and career thoughts. *Journal of Psychology, 142*, 21–35.

Strelau, J. (1998). *Psychologia temperamentu* [Psychology of temperament]. Warszawa: Wydawnictwo Naukowe PWN.

Strelau, J. (2006). *Temperament jako regulator zachowania. Z perspektywy półwiecza badań* [Temperament as a regulator of behavior. From the perspective of half a century of research]. Gdańsk: Gdańskie Wydawnictwo Psychologiczne.

Strong, E.K. (1943). *The vocational interests of men and women.* Stanford. CA: Stanford University Press.

Super, D.E. (1957). *The psychology of careers.* New York: Harper & Brothers.

Super, D.E. (1980). A life-span, life-space approach to career development. *Journal of Vocational Behavior, 16*, 282–298.

Super, D.E. (1972). *Psychologia zainteresowań* [Psychology of interests]. Warszawa: PWN.

Super, D.E. (1984). Career and life development. In: D. Brown, L. Brooks (ed.). *Career Choice and Development* (pp. 192–234). San Francisco. Washington. London: Jossey-Bass Publishers.

Super, D.E., & Bohn, M. (1971). *Occupational psychology.* London: Tavistock Publication Limited.

Super, D.E., & Nevill, D.D. (1984). Work role salience as a determinant of career maturity in high school students. *Journal of Vocational Behavior, 25*, 30–44.

Suświłło, M. (2004). *Inteligencje wielorakie w nowoczesnym kształceniu* [Multiple intelligence in modern edycation]. Olsztyn: Wydawnictwo Uniwersytetu Warmińsko-Mazurskiego.

Szcześniak, M., & Rondon, G. (2012). Pokolenie ani-ani: o młodzieży, która nie uczy się, nie pracuje i nie dba o samokształcenie [Generation neither-nor: about: young people who do not learn, do not work and do not care about self-education], *Psychologia Społeczna, 63*, 241–251.

Tabachnick, B.G., & Fidel L.S. (2007). *Using Multivariate Statistics.* Boston: Pearson Education. Inc.

Tiedeman, D.V. & O'Hara, R.P. (1963). *Career Development: Choice and Adjustment. Differentiation and Integration in Career Development.* New York: College Entrance Examination Board.

Tieger, P.D., & Barron-Tieger, B. (1999). *Rób to do czego jesteś stworzony* [Do what you are]. Warszawa: Studio EMKA.

Torre, L., Navarrete, H., Muriel, P.M., Macía, M.J., & Balslev, H. (eds.). (2008). *Enciclopedia de las plantas Útiles del Ecuador.* Herbario QCA de la Escuela de Ciencias Biológicas de la Pontificia Universidad Católica del Ecuador & Herbario AAU del departamento de Ciencias Biológicas de la Universidad de Aarhus. Quito: Quito & Aarhus.

Torres, M.R. (2005) *Illiteracy and literacy education in Ecuador: Options for policy and practice. Case study prepared at the request of UNESCO for inclusion in the 2005.* Education for All Global Monitoring Report. Quito: Fronesis Institute www.fronesis.org.

Turner, M. (1996). *Death is the mother of beauty: mind, metaphor, criticism.* Chicago: Chicago University Press.

Tyszkowa, M. (1990). *Zdolności, osobowość i działalność uczniów* [Abilities, personality and activity of students]. Warszawa: PWN.

UNESCO (2010). *Textos fundamentales de la Convención para la Salvaguardia del Patrimonio Cultural Inmaterial de 2003,* Oxford: UNESCO Print.

Valsiner, J. (2012). *The Oxford Handbook of Culture.* Oxford: Oxford University Press.

Vernon, P.E. (1979). *Intelligence: Heredity and environment.* San Francisco: W.H. Freeman & Company.

Villwock, J.D., Schnitzen, J.P., & Carbonari, J.P. (1976). Holland's personality constructs as predictors of stability of choice. *Journal of Vocational Behavior, 9,* 77–85.

Walsh, W.B., & Osipow, S.H (eds.). (1988). *Career decision making.* Hilsdale, NJ: Lawrence Erlbaum Associates.

Wechsler, D. (1944). *The measurement of adult intelligence.* Baltimore: Williams & Wilkin.

Weinrach, S.G. (1984). Determinants of vocational choice: Holland's theory. In: D. Brown, L. Brooks, (eds.), *Career Choice and Development* (pp. 61–93). San Francisco, Washington, London: Jossey-Bass Publishers.

Weiss, D., Freund, A.M., & Wiese, B.S. (2012). Mastering developmental transitions in young and middle adulthood: The Interplay of openness to experience and traditional gender ideology on women's self-efficacy and subjective well-being. *Developmental Psychology, 48,* 1774–1784.

Whorf, L. (2002). *Język, myśl i rzeczywistość* [Language, thought and reality]. Warszawa: Wydawnictwo KR.

Whorf, B.L. (1956). *Language, thought and reality: Selective writings of Benjamin Lee Whorf.* New York: Wiley.

Wiley, M.O., & Magoon, T.M. (1982). Holland high-point social types: Is consistency related to persistent and achievement? *Journal of Vocational Behavior, 20,* 14–21.

Wittgenstein, L. (2000). *Dociekania filozoficzne* [Philosophical inquiries] (transl. B. Wolniewicz). Warszawa: Wydawnictwo Naukowe PWN.

Wołońciej, M.T. (2012). *Kultura pracy i organizacji w przysłowiach polskich i niemieckich. Perspektywa psychologiczna* [Culture of work and organizations in Polish and German proverbs. Psychological perspective]. Lublin Towarzystwo Naukowe KUL.

Wołońciej, M.T., & Gellert. F.J. (2009). Contemporary nomads at work: a new trend in work culture. *Journal for Perspectives on Economic Political and Social Integration, 9,* 72–94.

Yang, Y., & Barth, J. (2015). Gender differences in STEM undergraduates' vocational interests undergraduates' vocational interests: People–thing orientation and goal affordances. *Journal of Vocational Behavior, 91,* 65–75.

Zawadzki, B., & Strelau, J. (1997). *Formalna charakterystyka zachowania – kwestionariusz temperamentu (FCZ-KT). Podręcznik* [Formal behavioral characteristics – temperament questionnaire (FCZ-KT). Manual]. Warszawa: Pracowania Testów Psychologicznych PTP.

Appendices

Appendix 1. The pilot version of the IPPJ (120 items)

Secretaria de Educación Superior,
Ciencia, Tecnología e Innovación.

INVENTARIO DE INTERESES PROFESIONALES DE JOVENES (IIPJ)

Escriba su número de cedula:

Proceso de evalución 2014

INVENTARIO DE PREFERENCIAS PROFESIONALES PARA JÓVENES (IPPJ)

Elaboración: Ph. D. Mariusz Wołońciej

MANUAL DE INSTRUCCIÓN

La encuesta que tienes en tus manos contiene 126 afirmaciones sobre aficiones y preferencias. Lee muy atentamente cada frase y responde sinceramente a la siguiente pregunta: ¿Hasta qué punto este enunciado me caracteriza? Elije la respuesta marcando el número adecuado en la burbuja. en la hoja de respuestas que tienes por separado. Puedes elegir una de las siguientes respuestas:

①②③④⑤

1. Totalmente en **desacuerdo**
2. En desacuerdo
3. Es difícil decidir
4. De acuerdo
5. Totalmente de **acuerdo**

Importante: Marca las afirmaciones **de este cuadernillo de ítems** que son poco claras. indicando con un círculo el número correspondiente como en el siguiente ejemplo:

Ejemplo	1. Me gustaría hacer publicidad televisiva.

1.	En la institución educativa me gusta actuar en una obra teatro juvenil.
2.	En el futuro. me gustaría dirigir mi propia empresa.
3.	En la escuela me gustan la matemática. la física y la informática.
4.	Me gusta llevar mis cuadernos de manera ordenada y limpia.
5.	Soy muy realista a los problemas del medio ambiente.
6.	Me gustaría cuidar personas con enfermedades mentales.
7.	Me gustaría hacer publicidad televisiva.
8.	En mi futuro trabajo. me gustaría sentirme independiente.
9.	Me gustaría manejar equipos técnicos de nueva generación.
10.	Mi actitud frente al trabajo y al aprendizaje es ordenada y sistemática.
11.	En mi futuro trabajo me gustaría tener contacto con animales.
12.	A veces en la escuela soluciono conflictos de mis compañeros y compañeras.
13.	Sé tocar un instrumento musical o me gustaría aprender.
14.	Me siento bien y me las arreglo cuando tengo que organizar el trabajo de mis compañeros y compañeras. fijarles tareas y comprobar si han sido realizadas.

15.	Me gusta resolver tareas y problemas "no comunes".
16.	Aceptaría un trabajo. donde pudiera comprobar que no hay errores en una documentación.
17.	Me gusta realizar pequeñas reparaciones de equipos electrodomésticos.
18.	Me gustaría encargarme de la inclusión social de niños y jóvenes.
19.	En el futuro. me gustaría escribir poemas. guiones de películas o de juegos de video.
20.	Me gusta tomar la palabra en diferentes discusiones y convencer a la gente.
21.	Me gusta mucho participar en competiciones escolares de diferentes asignaturas.
22.	Con exactitud contesto los formularios y no es una actividad aburrida para mí.
23.	Me gustaría trabajar en el servicio técnico de una empresa.
24.	Me gusta mucho participar en organizaciones no gubernamentales como la Cruz Roja o una organización de jóvenes exploradores.
25.	Me gusta ver exposiciones de esculturas. de pintura o fotografías.
26.	Sé animar a mis compañeros y compañeras a que participen en diversas actividades.
27.	Mis compañeros y compañeras me consideran una persona ingeniosa.
28.	En mi puesto de trabajo me gustaría trabajar según normas estrictamente definidas.
29.	En la escuela me gustan las actividades prácticas y técnicas.
30.	Me gusta ayudar a mis compañeros y compañeras a aprender y hacer sus deberes.
31.	Me gusta participar en clases de arte. música o de literatura.
32.	En las actividades de grupo fomento el liderazgo y la coordinación.
33.	Me gusta pensar en las causas y consecuencias de los acontecimientos.
34.	Me gustaría tener un trabajo donde tenga que realizar tareas muy precisas.
35.	Me interesan los aspectos técnicos de la industria automovilística.
36.	Me sentiría bien en un trabajo que requiriera de mí. mucha paciencia y comprensión frente a los demás.
37.	En la institución educativa me gusta escribir composiciones con ¨temas abiertos¨.
38.	Me gusta ver programas informativos sobre la situación económica actual en mi país y en el mundo.
39.	Me gusta analizar los problemas desde diferentes puntos de vista.
40.	Me gusta las tareas en las que puedo solucionar o realizar según indicaciones precisas.
41.	Me gusta mucho la carpintería.
42.	Me gusta participar en labores sociales.
43.	Me gusta cambiar el aspecto de otras personas o habitaciones.
44.	Sé dar a los demás instrucciones y consejos claros.
45.	El trabajo científico me parece muy interesante.
46.	En mi trabajo me gustaría digitar textos en un computador.
47.	Dibujar esquemas o proyectos de equipos es una tarea interesante y agradable para mí.
48.	Me sentiría bien. ayudando a los demás a comprenderse.
49.	Me interesan las revistas dedicadas al arte. a los muebles y a la arquitectura.
50.	Me gustaría trabajar en un centro de investigación o en un laboratorio.

51. Me gustaría tener un trabajo tranquilo con reglas o instrucciones claras.
52. Me interesa la agricultura ecológica.
53. Con muchas ganas y gran dedicación enseñaría a los jóvenes cómo evitar ciertas adicciones.
54. Me interesa la peluquería. la cosmetología o el arte del maquillaje.
55. En mi tiempo libre. me gusta hacer rompecabezas. jeroglíficos. resolver problemas lógicos o jugar al ajedrez.
56. Me gusta respetar y cumplir las fechas límites.
57. De niño o niña me gustaba desarmar mis juguetes.
58. Me gustaría dirigir el trabajo de un grupo que haga proyectos.
59. En el futuro me gustaría trabajar con niños y niñas.
60. Me gusta diseñar vestuarios.
61. Me gusta pensar en cómo perfeccionar el funcionamiento de diferentes equipos.
62. No me gustan situaciones que conllevan un riesgo.
63. Me gustaría arreglar o componer diferentes máquinas y equipos.
64. Me interesa cómo se dirigen las empresas y organizaciones.
65. Me gustaría ayudar a la gente a resolver sus problemas sociales.
66. Mi pasión es el baile. me gusta practicar y actuar en público.
67. Me interesan los descubrimientos científicos y las nuevas invenciones.
68. En mi mesa de estudios me gusta tener todo perfectamente ordenado.
69. Me gustaría participar activamente en actividades a favor del medio ambiente.
70. Con muchas ganas aceptaría el cargo de director o gerente de una empresa.
71. Me gusta pensar en diferentes aspectos del comportamiento humano.
72. Me gustaría tocar en un grupo musical o en una orquesta.
73. Me gustaría programar. diseñar nuevos programas informáticos.
74. Me gusta planificar y controlar bien mis gastos.
75. Me gustaría aprender a hacer dibujos técnicos.
76. Me gustaría desempeñar un papel responsable en el gobierno escolar o de la clase.
77. Mis compañeros y compañeras les agrada dirigirse a mí. con sus problemas.
78. Me gusta pasar mi tiempo libre en clases de baile.
79. Me gusta hacer experimentos y observar cómo se hacen.
80. Me interesa la organización de una secretaría o de una oficina.
81. Conozco el diseño y el funcionamiento del computador.
82. Me gusta tomar la iniciativa.
83. Me gusta cooperar con la gente y con los compañeros o compañeras de la institución educativa.
84. Me gustaría que en mi futuro trabajo me permitieran expresar mis ideas y emociones.
85. Me gusta ver los programas de televisión dedicados a las novedades científicas.
86. En mi trabajo podría hacer cálculos estadísticos y llevar la documentación.

87. Cuando paseo en las montañas o en un bosque. me detengo para ver de cerca plantas y árboles que no conozco.

88. En la institución educativa me gusta mucho participar en la organización de fiestas y excursiones.

89. En mi futuro trabajo me gustaría ayudar a personas con discapacidades.

90. Me gustaría crear o componer algún tipo de música.

91. Me aburre la rutina y la repetitividad de algunas actividades.

92. Me gustaría aprender la contabilidad y sus reglas.

93. Me gustaría diseñar o arreglar máquinas y equipos modernos.

94. Me gusta asumir la responsabilidad por las tareas que dirijo.

95. Me interesa leer artículos y libros sobre las relaciones interpersonales.

96. Me gustaría hacer dibujos para libros o crear carteles.

97. Me interesan nuevas ramas de la ciencia. tales como la genética o la biotecnología.

98. Por las tardes. me gusta planear el trabajo que tengo que hacer al día siguiente.

99. En el futuro. me gustaría trabajar con herramientas y equipos técnicos.

100. Me gustaría desempeñar el papel de presidente de la clase.

101. Me gustaría trabajar en un centro de ayuda telefónica para jóvenes.

102. En el futuro me gustaría expresarme mediante una actividad creativa como: la pintura. el dibujo. la escultura. el baile o el canto.

103. Me gustaría realizar estudios y descubrir la vacuna contra una enfermedad grave.

104. Me gusta organizar mi trabajo día a día y para la semana.

105. Me gustaría trabajar en un taller de mecánica automotriz.

106. Me gustaría liderar un grupo de mis compañeros y compañeras para organizar una fiesta escolar.

107. Me sentiría bien ayudando a personas nerviosas o tristes por algún motivo.

108. Me gustaría crear la coreografía de un baile moderno.

109. Me gustaría realizar estudios sobre el funcionamiento del cerebro.

110. Hago bien las tareas que requieren un trabajo sistemático y ordenado.

111. Me gusta aprender cómo funcionan los equipos técnicos.

112. Me gustaría aprender a liderar a la gente para gestionar sus acciones.

113. Soy capaz de dedicar mi tiempo a mis compañeros y compañeras que lo necesitan.

114. Me gustaría actuar en un escenario: bailar. cantar e interpretar papeles.

115. Me interesan nuevas ramas de la ciencia y la tecnología.

116. Me gusta tener ordenada mi habitación y mi mesa de estudios.

117. Me gustan las tareas que requieren habilidades manuales.

118. Me gustaría tener un trabajo donde tome decisiones y planear acciones para otras personas.

119. Me gustaría ayudar a otras personas a solucionar sus problemas.

120. Me gusta dirigir el trabajo de los demás.

121. Me gusta participar en clases arte. de música o de literatura.

122. En las actividades de grupo fomento el liderazgo y la coordinación.

123. Me gusta pensar en las causas y consecuencias de los acontecimientos.
124. Me gustaría tener un trabajo donde tenga que realizar tareas muy precisas.
125. Me interesan los aspectos técnicos de la industria automovilística.
126. Me sentiría bien en un trabajo que requiriera de mí mucha paciencia y comprensión frente a los demás.

¿Qué te gustó en el <u>cuestionario</u>?

....

....

....

....

¿Qué no te gustó en el <u>cuestionario</u>?

....

....

....

....

Appendix 2. Answer sheet for the pilot version IPPJ (120 items)

HOJA DE RESPUESTAS INVENTARIO DE PREFERENCIAS PROFESIONALES PARA JOVENES (IPPJ)

EJEMPLO DE LLENADO
CÉDULA

| 1 | 0 | 5 | 6 | 8 | 8 | 7 | 0 | 0 | 7 |

CÉDULA

Nombres:

Apellidos:

Edad: ⓪①②③④⑤⑥⑦⑧⑨   ⓪①②③④⑤⑥⑦⑧⑨   Sexo: F ◯   M ◯

Tipo de bachillerato:

Técnico ◯   Bachillerato General Unificado ◯   Artístico ◯   Bachillerato Internacional ◯

Zona de Residencia: Urbano ◯   Rural ◯

Provincia de nacimiento: ①②③④⑤⑥⑦⑧⑨⑩⑪⑫⑬⑭⑮⑯⑰⑱⑲⑳㉑㉒㉓㉔

Ocupación del padre: Ocupación de la madre:

¿En cuál profesión te gustaria trabajar en el futuro?:

CUADRO DE RESPUESTAS

Los codigos de 24 provincias
1.   Azuay
2.   Bolívar
3.   Cañar
4.   Carchi
5.   Chimborazo
6.   Cotopaxi
7.   El Oro
8.   Esmeraldas
9.   Galápagos
10. Guayas
11. Imbabura
12. Loja
13. Los Ríos
14. Manabí
15. Morona Santiago
16. Napo
17. Orellana
18. Pastaza
19. Pichincha
20. Santa Elena
21. Santo Domingo de los Tsáchilas
22. Sucumbíos
23. Tungurahua
24. Zamora Chinchipe

Appendix 3. The key of the pilot version scales (120 items)

Realistic: 5. 11. 17. 23. 29. 35. 41. 47. 53. 59. 65. 71. 77. 83. 89. 95. 101. 107. 113. 119
Investigative: 3. 9. 15. 21. 27. 33. 39. 45. 51. 57. 63. 69. 75. 81. 87. 93. 99. 105. 111. 117
Artistic: 1. 7. 13. 19. 25. 31. 37. 43. 49. 55. 61. 67. 73. 79. 85. 91. 97. 103. 109. 115
Social: 6. 12. 18. 24. 3. 36. 42. 48. 54. 6. 66. 72. 78. 84. 9. 96. 102. 108. 114. 120
Enterprising: 2. 8. 14. 2. 26. 32. 38. 44. 50. 56. 62. 68. 74. 8. 86. 92. 98. 104. 11. 116.
Conventional: 4. 1. 16. 22. 28. 34. 4. 46. 52. 58. 64. 7. 76. 82. 88. 94. 10. 106. 112. 118

Appendix 4. Items of the final version (60) with type codes after Factor Analysis of the pilot version (120)

Code	Items with the pilot version codes
R	R_17_I like making some small repairs of domestic equipment.
I	I_45_A scientific job seems very interesting to me.
A	A_13_I can play a musical instrument or I would like to learn how to do it.
S	S_6_I would like to take care of people with mental diseases.
E	E_14_It makes me feel good and I can manage the organization of my school mates' work. when I have to assi_n tasks to them and check out if they have been completed.
C	C_4_I like to keep my notebooks clean and well-organized.
R	R_23_I would like to work in the technical service of some company.
I	I_50_I would like to work in a research center or a laboratory.
A	A_19_In the future I would like to write poems. movie or games scripts.
S	S_24_I like participating in nongovernmental organizations. such as the Red Cross or a scout move_ent.
E	E_S_12_Sometimes at school I solve conflicts between my mates.˙
C	C_28_In my job I would like to work in accordance with some strictly defined rules.
R	R_35_I am interested in technical aspects of the automotive industry.
I	I_67_I like scientific discoveries and new inventions.
A	A_25_I would like to see school exhibits of sculpture. paintings and photographs.
S	S_42_I like taking part in social works.
E	E_32_In group activities I encourage leadership and coordination.
C	C_34_I would like to have a job where I could do some precise tasks.
R	R_47_Drawing schemes and group projects is a very nice and interesting task to me.
I	I_79_I like carrying out experiments and observing how they are carried out.
A	A_31_I like taking part in art. music and literature classes.
S	S_48_I would feel good helping people to understand each other.
E	E_20_I like having a word in different discussions and convincing people.
C	C_56_I like respecting and meeting deadlines.
R	R_99_In the future. I would like to work with tools and technical devices.
I	I_85_I like watching TV programs dedicated to scientific news.
A	A_49_I am interested in magazines about art. furniture and architecture.
S	S_53_With pleasure and dedication I would teach teenagers about how to avoid some addictions.
E	E_106_I would like to lead a group of my school mates in order to organize a school party
C	C_51_I would like to have a calm job with clear rules or instructions.

R	R_81_I know the way a computer is designed and the way it functions.
I	I_R_87_When walking in the mountains or in a forest. I stop to take a closer look at plants and trees that are new to me¨.
A	A_72_I would like to play in a music band or an orchestra.
S	S_59_In the future I would like to work with young boys and girls.
E	E_44_I can give instructions and advice to other people.
C	C_98_In the evenings. I like planning the work I have to do next day.
R	R_105_I would like to work in a car service station.
I	I_97_I am interested in new branches of science. such as genetics and biotechnology.
A	A_90_I would like to create or compose some kind of music.
S	S_65_I would like to help people to solve their social problems.
E	E_100_I would like to have the role of a class president.
C	C_68_On my desk I like to have everything perfectly organized.
R	R_75_I would like to learn how to make technical drawings.
I	I_103_I would like to carry out researches and discover the vaccine for a serious disease.
A	A_96_I would like to make drawings for book or create posters.
S	S_89_In my future job I would like to help disabled people.
E	E_118_I would like to have a job where I could make decisions and plan actions for other people.
C	C_74_I like to plan and control adequately my expenses.
R	R_111_I like learning how technical devices work.
I	I_109_I would like to study the brain functioning.
A	A_102_In the future. I would like to express myself through a creative activity. such as painting. drawing. sculpture. dancing or singing.
S	S_101_I would like to work in a telephone assistance center for teenagers.
E	E_112_I would like to learn how to lead a group of people in order to control their actions.
C	C_116_I like to have my desk and my room well-organized.
R	R_93_I would like to design and mend machines and modern devices.
I	I_115_I am interested in new branches of science and technology.
A	A_114_I would like to act in performances: to dance, sing or interpret some roles.
S	S_107_I would feel good at helping people who are nervous or sad for some reason.
E	E_120_I like to control the work of other people.
C	C_104_I like organizing my work every day and for the whole week.

˙ Though this item was considered in the pilot version as the Social type, however on the basis of the Factor Analysis results was added to the Entreprenerial type items.

¨ Though this item was considered in the pilot version as the Realistic type, however on the basis of the Factor Analysis results was added to the Investigative type items.

The code of each item consists of the number of the item in the pilot version (120 items) and the letter denotes the code of the RIASEC scale (eg. S_107 – Social)

Remark
1. After the Factor Analysis the Item S12 (Social) from the pilot version (120 items) was finally included in the E scale (Enterprising)
2. The the Factor Analysis the item R87 (Realistic) from the pilot version (120 items) was finally included in the I scale (Investigative)

Appendix 5. The final version of the INVENTARIO DE PREFERENCIAS PROFESIONALES DE JÓVENES (IPPJ) (60 items)

Secretaria de Educación Superior,
Ciencia, Tecnología e Innovación.

Proceso de evalución 2014

MANUAL DE INSTRUCCIÓN

La encuesta que tienes en tus manos contiene 60 afirmaciones sobre aficiones y preferencias. Lee muy atentamente cada frase y responde sinceramente a la siguiente pregunta: ¿Hasta qué punto este enunciado me caracteriza? Elije la respuesta marcando el número adecuado en la burbuja. en la hoja de respuestas que tienes por separado. Puedes elegir una de las siguientes respuestas:

1. *Totalmente en **desacuerdo***
2. *En desacuerdo*
3. *Es difícil decidir*
4. *De acuerdo*
5. *Totalmente de **acuerdo***

1	Me gusta realizar pequeñas reparaciones de equipos electrodomésticos.	
2	El trabajo científico me parece muy interesante.	
3	Sé tocar un instrumento musical o me gustaría aprender.	
4	Me gustaría cuidar personas con enfermedades mentales.	
5	Me siento bien y me las arreglo cuando tengo que organizar el trabajo de mis compañeros y compañeras, fijarles tareas y comprobar si han sido realizadas.	
6	Me gusta llevar mis cuadernos de manera ordenada y limpia.	
7	Me gustaría trabajar en el servicio técnico de una empresa.	
8	Me gustaría trabajar en un centro de investigación o en un laboratorio.	
9	En el future, me gustaría escribir poemas, guiones de películas o de juegos de video.	
10	Me gusta mucho participar en organizaciones no gubernamentales como la Cruz Roja o una organización de jóvenes exploradores.	
11	A veces en la escuela soluciono conflictos de mis compañeros y compañeras.	
12	En mi puesto de trabajo me gustaría trabajar según normas estrictamente definidas.	
13	Me interesan los aspectos técnicos de la industria automovilística.	
14	Me interesan los descubrimientos científicos y las nuevas invenciones.	
15	Me gusta ver exposiciones de esculturas, de pintura o fotografías.	
16	Me gusta participar en labores sociales.	
17	En las actividades de grupo fomento el liderazgo y la coordinación.	
18	Me gustaría tener un trabajo donde tenga que realizar tareas muy precisas.	
19	Dibujar esquemas o proyectos de equipos es una tarea interesante y agradable para mí.	
20	Me gusta hacer experimentos y observar cómo se hacen.	
21	Me gusta participar en clases de arte, música o de literatura.	

22	Me sentiría bien, ayudando a los demás a comprenderse.	
23	Me gusta tomar la palabra en diferentes discusiones y convencer a la gente.	
24	Me gusta respetar y cumplir las fechas límites.	
25	En el futuro, me gustaría trabajar con herramientas y equipos técnicos.	
26	Me gusta ver los programas de televisión dedicados a las novedades científicas.	
27	Me interesan las revistas dedicadas al arte. a los muebles y a la arquitectura.	
28	Con muchas ganas y gran dedicación enseñaría a los jóvenes cómo evitar ciertas adicciones.	
29	Me gustaría liderar un grupo de mis compañeros y compañeras para organizar una fiesta escolar.	
30	Me gustaría tener un trabajo tranquilo con reglas o instrucciones claras.	
31	Conozco el diseño y el funcionamiento del computador.	
32	Cuando paseo en las montañas o en un bosque, me detengo para ver de cerca plantas y árboles que no conozco.	
33	Me gustaría tocar en un grupo musical o en una orquesta.	
34	En el futuro me gustaría trabajar con niños y niñas.	
35	Sé dar a los demás instrucciones y consejos claros.	
36	Por las tardes, me gusta planear el trabajo que tengo que hacer al día siguiente.	
37	Me gustaría trabajar en un taller de mecánica automotriz.	
38	Me interesan nuevas ramas de la ciencia, tales como la genética o la biotecnología.	
39	Me gustaría crear o componer algún tipo de música.	
40	Me gustaría ayudar a la gente a resolver sus problemas sociales.	
41	Me gustaría desempeñar el papel de presidente de la clase.	
42	En mi mesa de estudios me gusta tener todo perfectamente ordenado.	
43	Me gustaría aprender a hacer dibujos técnicos.	
44	Me gustaría realizar estudios y descubrir la vacuna contra una enfermedad grave.	
45	Me gustaría hacer dibujos para libros o crear carteles.	
46	En mi futuro trabajo me gustaría ayudar a personas con discapacidades.	
47	Me gustaría tener un trabajo donde pudiera tomar decisiones y planear acciones para otras personas.	
48	Me gusta planificar y controlar bien mis gastos.	
49	Me gusta aprender cómo funcionan los equipos técnicos.	
50	Me gustaría realizar estudios sobre el funcionamiento del cerebro.	
51	En el futuro me gustaría expresarme mediante una actividad creativa como: la pintura, el dibujo, la escultura, el baile o el canto.	
52	Me gustaría trabajar en un centro de ayuda telefónica para jóvenes.	
53	Me gustaría aprender a liderar a la gente para gestionar sus acciones.	
54	Me gusta tener ordenada mi habitación y mi mesa de estudios.	
55	Me gustaría diseñar o arreglar máquinas y equipos modernos.	
56	Me interesan nuevas ramas de la ciencia y la tecnología.	

57	Me gustaría actuar en un escenario: bailar, cantar e interpretar papeles.	
58	Me sentiría bien ayudando a personas nerviosas o tristes por algún motivo.	
59	Me gusta dirigir el trabajo de los demás.	
60	Me gusta organizar mi trabajo día a día y para la semana.	

Appendix 6. The key of the IPPJ (final version)

R	I	A	S	E	C
1	2	3	4	5	6
7	8	9	10	11	12
13	14	15	16	17	18
19	20	21	22	23	24
25	26	27	28	29	30
31	32	33	34	35	36
37	38	39	40	41	42
43	44	45	46	47	48
49	50	51	52	53	54
55	56	57	58	59	60
RS Final score R …….	RS Final score I …….	RS Final score A …….	RS Final score S …….	RS Final score E …….	RS Final score C …….

Appendix 7. The translation of the IPPJ items from Spanish into English

No	Items in Castellano	Code	Items in English
1	Me gusta realizar pequeñas reparaciones de equipos electrodomésticos.	R	I like making some small repairs of domestic equipment.
2	El trabajo científico me parece muy interesante.	I	A scientific job seems very interesting to me.
3	Sé tocar un instrumento musical o me gustaría aprender.	A	I can play a musical instrument or I would like to learn how to do it.
4	Me gustaría cuidar personas con enfermedades mentales.	S	I would like to take care of people with mental diseases.
5	Me siento bien y me las arreglo cuando tengo que organizar el trabajo de mis compañeros y compañeras, fijarles tareas y comprobar si han sido realizadas.	E	It makes me feel good and I can manage the organization of my school mates' work when I have to assign tasks to them and check out if they have been completed.
6	Me gusta llevar mis cuadernos de manera ordenada y limpia.	C	I like to keep my notebooks clean and well-organized.
7	Me gustaría trabajar en el servicio técnico de una empresa.	R	I would like to work in the technical service of some company.
8	Me gustaría trabajar en un centro de investigación o en un laboratorio.	I	I would like to work in a research center or a laboratory.
9	En el futuro, me gustaría escribir poemas, guiones de películas o de juegos de video.	A	In the future I would like to write poems, movie or games scripts.
10	Me gusta mucho participar en organizaciones no gubernamentales como la Cruz Roja o una organización de jóvenes exploradores.	S	I like participating in nongovernmental organizations, such as the Red Cross or a scout movement.
11	A veces en la escuela soluciono conflictos de mis compañeros y compañeras.	E	Sometimes at school I solve conflicts between my mates.
12	En mi puesto de trabajo me gustaría trabajar según normas estrictamente definidas.	C	In my job I would like to work in accordance with some strictly defined rules.
13	Me interesan los aspectos técnicos de la industria automovilística.	R	I am interested in technical aspects of the automotive industry.
14	Me interesan los descubrimientos científicos y las nuevas invenciones.	I	I like scientific discoveries and new inventions.
15	Me gusta ver exposiciones de esculturas, de pintura o fotografías.	A	I would like to see school exhibits of sculpture, paintings and photographs.
16	Me gusta participar en labores sociales.	S	I like taking part in social works.
17	En las actividades de grupo fomento el liderazgo y la coordinación.	E	In group activities I encourage leadership and coordination.
18	Me gustaría tener un trabajo donde tenga que realizar tareas muy precisas.	C	I would like to have a job where I could do some precise tasks.

19	Dibujar esquemas o proyectos de equipos es una tarea interesante y agradable para mí.	R	Drawing schemes and group projects is a very nice and interesting task to me.
20	Me gusta hacer experimentos y observar cómo se hacen.	I	I like carrying out experiments, and observing how they are carried out.
21	Me gusta participar en clases de arte, música o de literatura.	A	I like taking part in art, music, and literature classes.
22	Me sentiría bien, ayudando a los demás a comprenderse.	S	I would feel good helping people to understand each other.
23	Me gusta tomar la palabra en diferentes discusiones y convencer a la gente.	E	I like having a word in different discussions and convincing people.
24	Me gusta respetar y cumplir las fechas límites.	C	I like respecting and meeting deadlines.
25	En el future, me gustaría trabajar con herramientas y equipos técnicos.	R	In the future. I would like to work with tools and technical devices.
26	Me gusta ver los programas de televisión dedicados a las novedades científicas.	I	I like watching TV programs dedicated to scientific news.
27	Me interesan las revistas dedicadas al arte. a los muebles y a la arquitectura.	A	I am interested in magazines about art, furniture and architecture.
28	Con muchas ganas y gran dedicación enseñaría a los jóvenes cómo evitar ciertas adicciones.	S	With pleasure and dedication I would teach teenagers about how to avoid some addictions.
29	Me gustaría liderar un grupo de mis compañeros y compañeras para organizar una fiesta escolar.	E	I would like to lead a group of my school mates in order to organize a school party
30	Me gustaría tener un trabajo tranquilo con reglas o instrucciones claras.	C	I would like to have a calm job with clear rules or instructions.
31	Conozco el diseño y el funcionamiento del computador.	R	I know the way a computer is designed and the way it functions.
32	Cuando paseo en las montañas o en un bosque, me detengo para ver de cerca plantas y árboles que no conozco.	I	When walking in the mountains or in a forest. I stop to take a closer look at plants and trees that are new to me.
33	Me gustaría tocar en un grupo musical o en una orquesta.	A	I would like to play in a music band or an orchestra.
34	En el futuro me gustaría trabajar con niños y niñas.	S	In the future I would like to work with young boys and girls.
35	Sé dar a los demás instrucciones y consejos claros.	E	I can give instructions and advice to other people.
36	Por las tardes, me gusta planear el trabajo que tengo que hacer al día siguiente.	C	In the evenings. I like planning the work I have to do next day.
37	Me gustaría trabajar en un taller de mecánica automotriz.	R	I would like to work in a car service station.
38	Me interesan nuevas ramas de la ciencia, tales como la genética o la biotecnología.	I	I am interested in new branches of science, such as genetics and biotechnology.
39	Me gustaría crear o componer algún tipo de música.	A	I would like to create or compose some kind of music.

40	Me gustaría ayudar a la gente a resolver sus problemas sociales.	S	I would like to help people to solve their social problems.
41	Me gustaría desempeñar el papel de presidente de la clase.	E	I would like to have the role of a class president.
42	En mi mesa de estudios me gusta tener todo perfectamente ordenado.	C	On my desk I like to have everything perfectly organized.
43	Me gustaría aprender a hacer dibujos técnicos.	R	I would like to learn how to make technical drawings.
44	Me gustaría realizar estudios y descubrir la vacuna contra una enfermedad grave.	I	I would like to carry out researches and discover the vaccine for a serious disease.
45	Me gustaría hacer dibujos para libros o crear carteles.	A	I would like to make drawings for book or create posters.
46	En mi futuro trabajo me gustaría ayudar a personas con discapacidades.	S	In my future job I would like to help disabled people.
47	Me gustaría tener un trabajo donde pudiera tomar decisiones y planear acciones para otras personas.	E	I would like to have a job where I could make decisions and plan actions for other people.
48	Me gusta planificar y controlar bien mis gastos.	C	I like to plan and control adequately my expenses.
49	Me gusta aprender cómo funcionan los equipos técnicos.	R	I like learning how technical devices work.
50	Me gustaría realizar estudios sobre el funcionamiento del cerebro.	I	I would like to study the brain functioning.
51	En el futuro me gustaría expresarme mediante una actividad creativa como: la pintura, el dibujo, la escultura, el baile o el canto.	A	In the future. I would like to express myself through a creative activity, such as painting, drawing, sculpture, dancing or singing.
52	Me gustaría trabajar en un centro de ayuda telefónica para jóvenes.	S	I would like to work in a telephone assistance center for teenagers.
53	Me gustaría aprender a liderar a la gente para gestionar sus acciones.	E	I would like to learn how to lead a group of people in order to control their actions.
54	Me gusta tener ordenada mi habitación y mi mesa de estudios.	C	I like to have my desk and my room well-organized.
55	Me gustaría diseñar o arreglar máquinas y equipos modernos.	R	I would like to design and mend machines and modern devices.
56	Me interesan nuevas ramas de la ciencia y la tecnología.	I	I am interested in new branches of science and technology.
57	Me gustaría actuar en un escenario: bailar, cantar e interpretar papeles.	A	I would like to act in performances: to dance, sing or interpret some roles.
58	Me sentiría bien ayudando a personas nerviosas o tristes por algún motivo.	S	I would feel good at helping people who are nervous or sad for some reason.
59	Me gusta dirigir el trabajo de los demás.	E	I like to control the work of other people.
60	Me gusta organizar mi trabajo día a día y para la semana.	C	I like organizing my work every day and for the whole week.

Appendix 8. Sten norms for vocational interests of girls (N = 962) (R, S, E, C scales)

STEN	Row results				STEN
	Realistic	Social	Enterprising	Conventional	
1	10–13	10–21	10–20	10–26	1
2	14–19	22–26	21–25	27–31	2
3	20–25	27–30	26–29	32–34	3
4	26–29	31–34	30–33	35–38	4
5	30–34	35–37	34–36	39–41	5
6	35–38	38–41	37–39	42–44	6
7	39–41	42–43	40–42	45–46	7
8	42–44	44–45	43–44	47–48	8
9	45–46	46–47	45–46	49	9
10	47–50	48–50	47–50	50	10

Appendix 9. Sten norms (R, S, E, C) for vocational interests of boys (N = 970)

STEN	Raw results				STEN
	Realistic	Social	Enterprising	Conventional	
1	11=23	10–15	10–21	10–25	1
2	24–28	16–20	22–25	26–30	2
3	29–32	21–24	26–29	31–34	3
4	33–36	25–28	30–32	35–37	4
5	37–39	29–32	33–35	38–40	5
6	40–42	33–36	36–38	41–43	6
7	43–44	37–39	39–41	44–46	7
8	45–46	40–42	42–43	47	8
9	47–48	43–44	44–45	48–49	9
10	49–50	45–50	46–50	50	10

Appendix 10. Sten norms (I, E) for vocational interests for girls and boys[1]
(N = 1932)

STEN	Raw results		STEN
	Investigative	Artistic	
1	10–17	10–16	1
2	18–23	17–22	2
3	24–28	23–27	3
4	29–33	28–31	4
5	34–37	32–35	5
6	38–41	36–39	6
7	42–44	40–42	7
8	45–46	43–45	8
9	47–48	46–47	9
10	49–50	48–50	10

[1] As diferences bitween boys and girls werde not significant statistically (discriminant analysis), the norms for the scales: Artistic and Investigative are presented at the same table.

Appendix 11. Sten norms for Holland's Differentiation indicators

STEN	Girls N = 962	Boys N = 970	STEN
1	1–4	1–3	1
2	5	4	2
3	6–7	5	3
4	8–9	5–7	4
5	10–11	8–10	5
6	12–15	11–13	6
7	16–21	14–18	7
8	22–27	19–23	8
9	28–34	24–30	9
10	35–45	31–45	10

Appendix 12. Sten norms for Iachan's Differentiation indicators

STEN	Girls N = 962	Boys N = 970	STEN
1	.00–.50	.00–.50	1
2	.51–.75	.50–.52	2
3	.76–.88	.53–.75	3
4	.89–1.25	.76–1.00	4
5	1.26–1.69	1.10–1.40	5
6	1.70–2.34	1.41–1.96	6
7	2.35–3.39	1.97–2.75	7
8	3.40–4.75	2.76–3.90	8
9	4.76–6.46	3.91–5.50	9
10	6.47–9.00	5.51–7.25	10

Appendix 13. Sten norms for Intensity Indicators

STEN	Girls N = 962	Boys N = 970	STEN
1	60–159	60–157	1
2	160–174	158–173	2
3	175–188	174–189	3
4	189–203	190–204	4
5	204–218	205–219	5
6	219–232	220–235	6
7	233–261	236–251	7
8	262–267	252–266	8
9	268–276	267–282	9
10	277–300	283–300	10

Appendix 14: The answer sheet: the table profile or/and the hexagon profile

STEN	Standardized results						STEN
	Realistic	Investigative	Artistic	Social	Enterprising	Conventional	
1							1
2							2
3							3
4							4
5							5
6							6
7							7
8							8
9							9
10							10

List of figures

List of tables

Mariusz Wołońciej. PhD; assistant professor at the Department of Experimental Psychology of the John Paul the II Catholic University of Lublin, Poland; He is interested in psychology of organization, work culture, cross-cultural communication and psychology in vocational guidance. His interdisciplinary investigations focus on the process of proverb thinking and organizational behavior existing in a culture. Experience and research run in Ecuador, Germany, Spain and Poland let him develop comparative studies in cross-cultural perspective.

Anna Paszkowska-Rogacz PhD, associated professor at the Department of Business Psychology and Career Counselling of the University of Lodz. In her scientific work a significant place was taken publications devoted to occupational psychology and vocational choice, mainly in the aspect of psychological conditioning and course of counseling process. She has about 50 published works including research reports, articles and books. She has experience in international projects on career counseling. She is a Member of International Association for Educational and Vocational Guidance.

REVIEWER
Adam Biela

INITIATING EDITOR
Urszula Dzieciątkowska

CO-TRANSLATOR
Patrick Lahey

LINGUISTIC EDITOR
Patrick Lahey

TYPESETTING
Munda – Maciej Torz

TECHNICAL EDITOR
Leonora Wojciechowska

COVER DESIGN
Katarzyna Turkowska

COVER IMAGE
© Depositphotos.com/ammmit

First Edition. W.08180.17.0.K

Publisher's sheets 12.3; printing sheets 11.0